Face to Face in the Workplace

Julie Cooper

Julie Cooper Adv DipEVG, Cert ACE, BPS:RQTU, Assoc IfL, Assoc CIPD

...is an innovative professional with a love of professional development issues and a special interest in helping others develop their one to one skills.

Her areas of expertise include assessment, employee development, education and training, guidance, and interview techniques.

20 years' consultancy experience has been gained through working with a broad range of public and private sector companies.

Julie has co-authored three other books, which have received excellent reviews:

- **The One to One Toolkit:** Tips and Strategies for Advisers, Coaches and Mentors *"I would definitely recommend this to anybody working with individuals on a 1-1 basis"*

- **The Groupwork Toolkit:** How to Convert Your One to One Advice Skills to Work with Groups *"The Group Work Tool Kit saved my life when I was doing my group work assessment"*

- **The Job Interview Toolkit:** Exercises to Get you Fit for Your Interview *"I found it very good. Clear, to the point, easy to read, great examples....."*

Face to Face in the Workplace

A handbook of strategies for effective discussions

The other
person
involved

Julie Cooper

Spring Development

Face to Face in the Workplace

© Copyright Julie Cooper 2012

Copy editing by the Oxford Word Salon

Cover design by 777ok and Dam Design

Illustration by Dave Nurney and Dam Design

ISBN 978-0-9559680-3-7

Published by Spring Development, an imprint of Careertrain Publishing

www.springdevelopment.net   www.careertrain.net

Printed and bound in Great Britain by the MPG Books Group

Note: The material contained in this book is set out in good faith for general guidance only and no liability can be accepted for loss or expense incurred as a result of relying in particular circumstances on statements made in this book.

Contents

Acknowledgements

I doubt I would have had the confidence or skill to write this book without the experience of co-authoring three books with Ann Reynolds. My deep appreciation goes to her for making this guide possible.

Many thanks go to Lynda Holt (www.lyndaholt.co.uk) and her Mastermind Group for her support, her inspiration, and for keeping me on track.

Special thanks go to Jane Armytage-Green of Athena Legal (www.athenalegal.co.uk) for advice on the content.

Jeremy Renals (www.oxfordwordsalon.com) made an excellent job of copy editing, coming up with great ideas, letting me know where I needed to improve and also coming up with a plan for the cover.

Debbie Mc Loughlin at DAM Design (www.damdesign.org.uk) took his idea and polished it into shape, as well as designing the Spring Development logo and branding.

Many thanks to Dave Nurney for the Topi cartoon too.

Lastly, thanks are due to the good folk of Banburyshire. It may be a fictitious county, but the people are not only real, but also warm and welcoming, making my relocation here a pleasure.

Foreword

We all acknowledge how important effective one-to-one communication is at the workplace, and can recognise when it goes well almost as easily as when it doesn't.

What's more difficult is to provide insights, understanding and approaches that can make workplace discussion more effective, and to do it in an approachable, practical way for anyone with an interest in the subject.

Julie Cooper's handbook accomplishes the feat in a helpful format that allows the reader to go into the right level of depth and detail for their particular needs, whether dipping into the "Basics" sections for a fresh look at listening skills, assertiveness etc. or ensuring that they are well versed in the planning and undertaking of formal interviews or conflict management.

A very useful additional tool for all of us involved in enhancing workplace communication, and the countless benefits such improvement can bring.

David Fogg

Principal, Oxford Business College

How to Use this Book

Welcome

This book is here to help you to get the best out of your one to one discussions at work.

If you are part of a team, responsible for managing others, or if you aspire to leadership, you are bound to come across most if not all of the topics described here.

Some chapters are about the formal one to one situations you will come across in the workplace, and some are about those other situations where planning and forethought will improve your chances of a positive, successful outcome.

Most of the time we have assumed that you are the more senior person, but of course sometimes the shoe is on the other foot, so where it seems fit there are a few words offered for when the tables are turned.

Talk is not cheap

There are many times in our working lives when we need to talk to each other.

Of course, this should be easy, right? We are all capable of holding a conversation. What else is there to it?

If only life were that simple! People are complex beings, with different personalities, opinions, perceptions, values, beliefs and experience.

Add to the mix the many reasons there may be for talking to someone, including both your agenda and theirs, and it becomes apparent that there are many different directions a conversation can take.

Much of the time we get the results we want, but other times we come away wishing that the outcome had been different, or with that nagging feeling that we haven't done as well as we hoped we would.

How this Handbook Works

This handbook doesn't have to be read from cover to cover.

You can dip in and out whenever you want to brush up and get organised for an imminent meeting.

It starts with the broad basics, and then addresses each type of conversation in turn.

First: the Basics

The Basics is the skills, knowledge and understanding you need to be an effective communicator.

It is wise to have a leaf through this section first. Some of it may be teaching your granny to suck eggs, but we all have gaps in our knowledge and experience, so it would be good to be aware and plug the gaps before you get in too deep.

For the rest of the book we are assuming that you have these basics covered.

Then: everything you wanted to know about discussions, interviews and conversations...

For the rest of the book we get down to a range of situations you'll want to manage well.

These chapters all follow the same format: **D.O.T.S., Good Practice, and Warning!**

D - Definition

Sometimes organisations use different language for the same thing; for example what you call an appraisal I might call a performance review.

Here you can check that you are in the right section for your needs.

O - Outcome

Also known as beginning with the end in mind. Here you can make sure that you know what you want to achieve, so that you have a focus when you start.

T - Think ahead

This will help you think about what to do ahead of the conversation, and alert you to any planning and preparation that should take place. Sometimes the planning is simply getting organised, at other times there are deeper questions to consider, so allow yourself thinking time.

S - Steps

Here you will find simple formats that can be used to give a structure to your conversation to make sure you cover the ground needed.

In some chapters the steps don't necessarily have to be covered in the order given, but will still give you key pointers on what to include.

Good Practice

After D.O.T.S. you will find Good Practice.

This covers more useful detail, often unwrapping the Think Ahead and Steps sections. There will be tips, techniques and ideas to help you on your way.

If anything in D.O.T.S. was not clear to you, read here for further explanation.

Warning!

Following the D.O.T.S. format should make most discussions plain sailing, but there are perils, pitfalls and possibly storms along the way that can be avoided with a little forethought.

So, every chapter also has a **Warning!** section, so that you can be aware of common difficulties and hopefully head them off at the pass.

Topi - The Other Person Involved

One more thing you need to know – let me introduce Topi.

The other person involved

This book is about one to one conversations. You are one of the two people involved. The other, for ease, we have called Topi.

Topi, you have probably worked out, is an acronym for **The Other Person Involved**.

In some chapters Topi is a woman, in others he is a man, but obviously Topi could be either at any time.

It is up to you to place Topi as the other person in your mind as you read the chapters.

What this Book is...

- **An easy to read,** brief guide to common discussions in the workplace.

- **A handy reference tool** for those of us who do not have the time or inclination to read extensively.

- **A practical source of frameworks,** checklists and strategies you can use to prepare for one to one meetings.

- **A good starting point for developing face to face** skills in the workplace, or reviewing your current practice.

- **A bit repetitive, sometimes**. Some of the topics overlap a little, so the content does too. Do look at similar chapters to the one that interests you, though.

  They may well contain a different technique or tip that is useful. Where another chapter might help you, we have cross referenced to it.

  Hopefully the consistent structure will help you find what you need quickly and easily.

What this Book is Not...

- **Designed to be read in one sitting.** You can certainly read The Basics and a couple of chapters that interest you to get a feel for how it works, though.

- **An academic tome.** It is written for the busy person to be able to access easily.

- **A thorough exploration of all the topics within.** All of the subject headings have had many books written about them. For some subjects, such as coaching or mentoring, we really are only touching the very small tip of a large iceberg. Some excellent books are in the biography, many more are available.

  Please do read further whenever you need more depth or breadth than is provided here.

- **A complete management training course.** Having effective face to face skills will take you a long way down the road, but it is not the be all and end all. For example, it won't teach you decision making skills or how to think laterally to generate ideas and options. Sometimes the conversation is only half the story, and you will need to explore elsewhere to complete your knowledge.

- **A manual on Human Resource (HR) practices or employment law.** Several of the chapters cover topics that have legal implications, so you really need to know where you stand. Whenever this is the case, you will be signposted to the relevant professionals that can help you.

  If your organisation is too small to have internal HR support, look out locally for independent HR professionals. There are many of them around, usually supporting a caseload of small companies, who either pay for their services on a retainer basis or use them as and when needed.

- **A rigid approach that is the only way to get results.** The frameworks are to guide you and give you confidence, and are not cast in stone. You may find that your personal style or even company procedures lead you down a different path.

  Being clear about why the conversation is taking place and what you are trying to achieve is more important than structure.

There we have it...

Dive in, the water is warm!

2

The Basics

This chapter looks at some aspects of talking and listening that you might not have thought about. Now's a good time to start.

Rapport

Several chapters in this book will advise you to set Topi at ease.

How will you do this?

Creating rapport is probably the most important factor. Rapport means getting on the same wavelength as someone else, so that they are comfortable around you and willing to carry on talking to you.

Sometimes we don't even need to think about how we create rapport because it comes naturally. We meet people who we instantly start chatting away to. Of course there are other times when we just don't 'get' the other person. They may be shy, not the type of person we're used to talking to, or just not presenting any behaviour that we know how to respond to.

Take a moment to think about someone new you have met recently.

- What happened in the very first moments of the conversation?

- How did you break the ice?

- Who spoke first?

- What was said?

- What body language were you both using?

- And the killer question... how are you the same as each other and how are you different?

The truth is that we find it easier to build relationships with people who share common ground, like subject matter, an experience, social class, gender, interests, personality, likes... the list is endless!

So, the obvious way forward is to find some.

The other important factor in building rapport is to be interested in the other person. Why should anyone engage with you if you appear to have no interest in them?

Here are some tips:

Verbal

- Use safe small talk that finds common ground (family and friends, hobbies, job, location). After all, you're both in the same place at the same time, so at the very least you have both had a journey to get there, and have an opinion of the surroundings.

- Use their name appropriately (beginning, middle, and end of conversation)

- Show empathy, see things from Topi's point of view. Even if you do not agree with their opinion, you can still try to understand where they are coming from.

- Choose suitable language. Make sure it is roughly at the same level as theirs, and beware of industry jargon and acronyms.

- Use verbal encouragers, such as *"uh huh"* or *"mm"*, etc to show that you are listening and interested.

- Be aware of your tone of voice and pace of your speech. If it is a complete mismatch with theirs, try slowing down, speeding up, lowering or raising your voice, or whatever it takes to be more in sync with them.

- The easiest way to introduce humour is to laugh at yourself!

Non verbal

- Maintain eye contact about 60% of the time. If you concentrate on them too hard, it can appear intimidating. If you spend your time while they are talking looking round the room, it will seem as if you are looking for escape routes to get out of the conversation. If you find it hard to maintain eye contact - and some people do - instead try looking at their ear lobe or nose – they won't be able to tell the difference. Don't try looking past them at the wall behind, they are likely to feel that you are looking through them.

- Lean towards them.

- Nod in agreement, or to encourage them to continue

- Tightly crossed arms can be seen as a barrier.

- Use touch appropriately. A light touch on the forearm or a pat on the shoulder are usually acceptable ways of showing someone we agree or are there for them. Touching, kissing and hugging are becoming increasingly the normal culture socially, and even in some workplaces. Be aware, however, that some people hate this! Always be aware of not invading someone's personal space, and take your lead from them. If in doubt, don't.

- Smile!

Bear in mind that if your verbal and non-verbal cues are not in harmony, the mixed message will cause confusion and distrust. When there is discord between the two, it is almost definite that your non-verbal behaviour will be believed. There is a bit more about this in the section on Body Language below.

Mirroring

Mirroring is a powerful way of building rapport.

It means subtly imitating the other person's body language. This is not a game of Simple Simon where you rigidly copy everything they do! Instead, you could adopt a similar pose, smile if they smile, be as relaxed or formal as they are. Use similar words and phrases to the ones they use.

If mirroring is something you have not been aware of until now, start by looking out for it any time you are around people. You will see that it occurs naturally much of the time.

It may feel a bit unnatural when you do it consciously, but be assured that the other person will not be aware of anything, other than feeling that you are getting on fine.

In fact, some say that if you master the art of mirroring a person you find difficult to understand, it can give you real clues to what is inside their head and what it is like to be them.

It can also be possible to persuade people to change their mood by mirroring their body language, and then slowly changing yours to reflect the mood you want to create. For example, if another person appears uptight (tense, rigid, unsmiling, folded arms), mirror this - and then gradually loosen up (drop your shoulders, lean back, unfold arms, smile) as the conversation develops. If they do not follow your lead, revert to the uptight body language and repeat the process. It may take a few attempts, but often you will win the other person round.

How not to do rapport

There are some behaviours that will send us running for the hills when we encounter them.

If you want to get rid of the of the other person quickly, you could :

- Talk at them, preferably all about you.

- Use the formal language you get in board papers but never in normal conversations.

- Be their parent, telling them what they must and should do, and what they ought to think.

- Disagree with them from the outset, without finding out why they hold their views.

- Be dogmatic.

- Present yourself as differently as you can to how they are presenting themselves.

- Be over familiar. Very quickly.

Self Awareness

You're working on strategies for discussions, but you may have missed something that will undermine the whole conversation: does the person you are talking to view you as a bumbling buffoon or an arrogant ass?

Of course they don't!

Or do they?

They must take a view of some sort. Do you know what it is? Do others see you as a quiet, calm rock? A lively, happy extrovert? A scheming, wily snake?

More importantly, what are they basing their opinions on?

Until you have a good understanding of how you come across to others, it is unlikely that you are in a position to adapt your behaviour to perform at your best or communicate effectively. It would be like planning a journey without knowing the starting destination. A knowledge of self is the beginning of all effective communication.

You cannot assume that you are self aware if you have never given the matter thought, or had input from people you trust to give you honest, objective feedback.

So what are we talking about here? Think about:

- **Your image.** What is your appearance saying about you? Is this the image you want to project?

- **Your behaviour.** Are you aware of the behaviours you choose? How do others interpret your behaviour? How much do you vary it in different situations?

- **Body language.** Are you conscious of your poise, how it changes and what it conveys?

- **Your speech.** What are your tone and pace like? Do you adjust your vocabulary for your audience? Do you use slang or jargon that befuddles the listener? What impression does the way you speak make on others – do you come across as reasonable? Soft? Pushy?

- **Your footprint.** By this we mean any trail you have left that gives others the opportunity to form an opinion about you.

  For example, this may be emails you have sent, stories that may be told, reports you have written, and people you associate with; all of these add to your reputation and impact.

So, how do people see you...?

A certain amount of self-awareness can be formed by reflection and self-analysis, for example thinking through the above questions will give you a starting point.

You can also canvas colleagues you trust to give you their thoughts when appropriate. For example, some of us are lucky enough to have a team awayday where honesty is high on the agenda, or can ask a line manager in a one to one meeting. You may also have a coach or a mentor who will give you a truthful answer.

...and is that how you see yourself?

Personality questionnaires are another good way of finding out about ourselves, and learning some of the psychology of behavioural style.

There are literally thousands of these available; do choose a reputable tool that has a scientific body of evidence behind it to back it up. If you complete one, maybe as part of a selection process, do ask for feedback.

The next section explains one of the popular theories that some personality tests use.

Personality Styles

You may be wondering if we really need to look at personality theory near the beginning of a book on one to one skills.

It must be possible to learn how to handle different conversations by memorising structures and models, mustn't it? After all, that is what the rest of book is about.

To an extent it is, but this, in itself, is not enough. A grasp of how people are different will help you build genuine working relationships, and master the art of adapting your style so that others can understand you more easily – and you can understand them.

The best 'you'

Note that we say "*adapting your style*", meaning operating within the range of behaviours that are within the scope of your personality, rather than trying to play the part of someone you are not.

You can only be yourself, and much has been written recently about the need to be authentic and genuine in our dealings with others. Others will find it hard to trust you if they sense that you are play acting and are not being true to yourself in any way.

Yet we can all learn new behaviours, modify and grow. The goal here is to be The Best You possible.

Do remember that personality and behaviour style are not static. We all have a range we can operate within, and we change and adapt as we mature and deal with all that life throws at us. A common trap is to label ourselves with traits we had when we were young or inexperienced, such as shy or forgetful, and then we continue to believe these things about ourselves even when life has long since taught us to behave differently.

Take a moment to consider how you label yourself, or how others label you. Does the tag still hold true? What are you really like these days?

The Big Five

There are many different theories of personality that have been used to underpin behavioural style questionnaires. Even psychologists can't agree on a definitive framework, so don't expect to know it all overnight!

Here are the bare bones of one of the most popular theories that is used: The Big Five.

The Big Five is a set of scales you can measure aspects of your personality against:

- **Openness**
- **Conscientiousness**
- **Extraversion**
- **Agreeableness**
- **Neuroticism**

First of all, you need to start with yourself. Use the framework to consider where you fit in each of the five scales. Once you have given it some thought you can ask people you trust to tell you where they would place you, and their reasons.

You can also think about where you feel people you know fit in. Are those you are close to similar in style to you? What about the person you struggle to get on with? Can you see where you are the same and where you are different? You might begin to see why personality clashes occur!

Behaviours that you see at either end of the scale are described below. Of course, in reality most of us fall somewhere between the two most of the time, and exactly where depends on the situation. Identifying which you are likely to lean towards is helpful; if you think you do 'fit' at the ends of several scales it is possible that you have a strong personality.

Is that true? Which words portray you?

Openness to Experience

Low ←   → High

- Down-to-earth
- Closed off
- Resistant to change
- Conventional
- Straightforward
- Traditional
- Likes familiarity
- Step-by-step thinking

- Appreciation of art
- Curiosity
- Imaginative
- Creative
- Open to new ideas,
- In touch with feelings
- Likes variety of experience

Conscientiousness

Low ←   → High

- Spontaneous
- Laid back
- Less driven by success
- Disorganised
- Procrastination
- Impulsive
- Here and now focus

- Attention to detail
- Always prepared
- Likes order
- Perfectionist
- Self discipline
- Careful
- Dutiful

Extraversion

Low ←   → **High**

- Low key
- Needing own space
- Depth of interests
- Happy with own company
- Think before speaking
- Reserved
- Prefer written communication

- Enthusiastic
- Action oriented
- Needing stimulation
- Energetic
- Sociable
- Speak before thinking
- Breadth of interests

Agreeableness

Low ←   → **High**

- Sceptical
- Stubborn
- Less interested in others
- Distrustful
- Task oriented
- Independent
- Not afraid to be unpopular

- Considerate
- Friendly
- Generous
- Helpful, willing to compromise
- Trusting
- Compassionate
- Sympathetic

Neuroticism

Low ←   → **High**

- Calm
- Stable
- Tolerant
- Reserved
- Unemotional
- Composed
- Bounces back

- Emotionally reactive
- Low stress tolerance
- Prone to anxiety
- Highly strung
- Perceive threats
- Negativity
- Unstable

Many psychologists have subdivided these scales into further traits that you can research if you want to take understanding seriously. If you are interested please do read up further, there are plenty of resources on hand.

There are now free Big Five questionnaires available online which may be worth investigating, but they are not as comprehensive as established paid-for tests, which as a rule will give you far more feedback.

And this is important because...?

Having got as far as thinking about your own behavioural style, and that of those around you, it is time to turn our attention to the *"So what?"* question. How does being able to identify behavioural traits improve our communication?

The answer is that you can use it to predict how someone may react, how they prefer to behave, to decide, and to receive information.

You will have clues about the situations they find comfortable, and what is difficult for them. It gives you the opportunity to plan how best to approach the individual concerned.

You can ask yourself questions like:

- How might they respond?

- What emotions will they display?

- What will their fears and concerns be?

- What issues will they raise?

- What type of approach will make it easier for them to accept what I am saying?

- How can I adjust my behaviour to help them engage with me, and understand the message I am giving?

The more you ask yourself questions like these, the better you will get at having effective, meaningful one to one discussions. Other forms of communication will work better, too.

For example...

Say, for example, you need to ask a couple of team members, Sally and Ben, to give up a Saturday to work on a project that is behind schedule. Sally is near the top of the extraversion and neuroticism scale, whereas Ben is a conscientious introvert .

We can guess that Sally would rather you told her in person rather than sending an email – she likes to talk to face to face. Ben, on the other hand, would probably like the opportunity to reflect on the content of an email before he gives you his considered response.

Sally is likely to be persuaded to work the Saturday if you give her the opportunity to express her emotions, and then show her how it will be a chance to stimulate the team into action. Ben would much rather hear that it will mean the team's work will be accurate and on target.

Both are true; it's a case of tuning in to what is important to the other person and presenting the information in a manner that they find easy to engage with. By the way, Ben would rather be out of earshot when you tell Sally. He would rather concentrate on his work without be disturbed by her initial outburst!

Assertive Behaviour

It is also worth being able to recognise your behavioural style in terms of the assertiveness model.

Being assertive means standing up for our own rights, but also taking into account the rights of others. We have a moral responsibility to behave in a way that does not intimidate or scare others – but also to not let them treat us badly.

Our goal is that we behave assertively in all our conversations, but that is not always the case. Take a moment to think about how you act in difficult situations. We all use different types of behaviour depending on the circumstance.

To successfully change a situation, you need to be aware of the type of behaviour you would unconsciously use, and consciously change your behaviour to the most appropriate type.

There are four types of behaviour below. How would you categorise yourself under pressure using this framework? How about your colleagues?

Aggressive

- Wins at the expense of others.

- Concerned with their own needs, not the needs of others.

- Often blunt, loud, interrupting, invading personal space.

- Might be sarcastic, critical or patronising.

- It is never their fault.

- Knows that they are most important, although often has little real self-esteem.

Passive

- Often says little, avoids eye contact, speaks hesitantly, quietly, or just agrees.

- Avoids conflict, does not express their feelings.

- Worried about what others may think of them.

- Doormat tendencies, gives in easily to please others.

- Fails to stand up for their rights.

- Apologetic, puts themselves down, may appear vague or indecisive.

Manipulative

- Wants to get even without confrontation.

- Uses emotional blackmail, making others feel guilty for not recognising their needs.

- Acts like a martyr, long suffering, uses gestures like rolling eyes rather than words.

- Uses indirect means get their own way.

- Body language may be in contrast to words, e.g. sighing while saying yes.

- Does not trust anyone, including themself.

Assertive

- Open, honest and direct communication.

- Stand up for themselves, but also respects the rights of others.

- Willing to compromise while looking for a win/win situation.

- Not dependent on others for approval, has self esteem.

- Knows their own needs, and accepts their own positive and negative qualities.

- Listens to others, shows understanding and acceptance.

Many of the suggestions you will find in the chapters that follow reflect assertive behaviour, as it underpins successful relationships.

No doubt we all aim to behave assertively, but most of us have areas in our lives where we slip into other modes. Recognising your own weak spots, and the impact on others involved, is important to our success in building relationships.

Behaving assertively

These two techniques can help you with your assertive behaviour:

Acknowledgement

This is simple but powerful, an essential part of assertive behaviour. It is often overlooked, though, so you may find it also mentioned elsewhere in this book.

We all appreciate it if we know we have been heard. We often feel better, even if the situation has not changed.

Find a way that suits your personal style to let Topi know that you are aware of her **emotion** and **situation.** You will need to back this up with active listening and appropriate body language.

Do not just trot out glib phrases, for example, do not say, "*I hear what you are saying*" unless you do! Here are some examples:

"*I appreciate the difficulty you are in...*"

"*I can see that you are frustrated at the lack of progress...*"

"*I realise that the workload is causing you to feel under pressure...*"

Broken record

This is a simple technique that you use when either you feel that you are not being heard, or the other person keeps muddying the field by bringing in side issues or irrelevancies that deflect from the purpose of the discussion.

For example, someone might say something like, *"...and another thing, you were late again yesterday, no wonder that report was not on my desk..."* or *"...you always get upset when the heat is on, just like that time when..."*. This may remind you of arguments when all manner of past injustices are raised.

The broken record technique requires you to not allow yourself to rise to the bait and be deflected form the topic in hand, and to keep repeating your point until you get acknowledgement from the other person.

This does not necessarily mean using exactly the same words every time, but it does involve being repetitious. Assertively deal with any attempted deflections, for example, you might say *"That is not the issue we are discussing here..."* *"Can we deal with that later? Right now I want to..."* *"Let's handle one thing at a time..."*

However you do it,

- Keep focused on what you are saying

- Be specific - do not use padding to weaken your statement

- Do not weaken! Repeat your message until it is heard

Credibility

The most valuable thing you bring to a conversation is your credibility, so it's worth taking a minute to think about it if you aim to be respected. If Topi does not perceive you or the organisation you represent as credible, it is unlikely that you will ever regain the lost ground.

So what do we mean by credibility?

The thesaurus lists believable, convincing, plausible, realistic, trustworthy, reliable and sincere. Honesty should also be added to the list. Consider the following points:

- What could indicate to Topi that you are not wholly reliable? If you can think of anything, what can be done to redress the balance?

- Be consistent. Say what you do and do what you say. Beware of jumping through hoops to please a colleague if you are not going to be able to repeat the exercise every time they ask you.

- Your credibility is dented when other people in your organisation do not follow through with their part of the job. Have an interest in the bigger picture.

- Is the timing right? Are both sides willing and able to participate in a reasonable frame of mind? Be sensitive; launching into full flow when Topi's mind is elsewhere will damage your credibility.

Explaining

The need to explain happens often. You may need to pass on a briefing, justify your course of action, or send information to another person.

How often does it happen that we think we have explained something clearly, yet it soon becomes obvious that the other person didn't get the message at all?

Begin at their starting point, not yours.

You can't build on Topi's knowledge if she has a flaky foundation that is likely to crumble when you lay the first brick. Use language she will understand, a pace she can follow and a style she can relate to.

Make sure you understand how much she already knows and if there are gaps in her knowledge.

Be aware of the difference between facts and assumptions, rumours, opinions and half-truths.

Why should Topi listen?

Before you start, think about Topi's motivation for listening to you. What is in it for her?

You may want to explain, but who is to say that Topi wants to be explained to? Just because it is on your agenda, it doesn't mean it is on hers.

If it is not obvious, it is a good idea to start by getting her buy in.

Think about it from her point of view and adjust your approach accordingly.

Back to the building blocks

Make sure you present the information or argument in a logical order that is easy to follow.

Many years ago I had a Saturday job in a small estate agents. The lovely, helpful lass that was leaving had one day to train me. She told me everything there was to know about estate agency at great speed in no particular order. It took me weeks to piece the information together into a coherent whole.

Have they understood?

Find a way to convince yourself that the other person has heard and understood, and will act where necessary.

Just asking *"Do you understand?"* is unlikely to be sufficient - you may discover in time that person erroneously thought they understood, or was too timid to own up.

Sometimes you can gauge understanding simply from conversation; the way it is flowing or the questions they ask show you that they have their wits about them.

At other times, you may need to take steps to reassure yourself. You can ask them questions like *"How will this affect us?"* Or *"What steps do think we should take next?"* That will probe and help you find out if they understood.

Another approach is to take responsibility by saying something like *"I'm not sure I explained that well, please could you tell me your understanding so that I can check if I have told you what you need to know?"*.

Listening

Make no mistake, listening is a vital yet often overlooked skill.

It is also a skill that can be developed.

It rarely comes naturally to us to give another person our full concentration. Many of us read the newspaper, check emails, or do the ironing while apparently listening to the radio, TV, family or friends.

Most of the time this is fine, but there are occasions where a higher quality of listening is needed.

Think of any normal conversation. You stop speaking, the other person starts. They stop speaking, so you start. Rarely is there a breath or a pause between speakers.

So the question is this: **Were you listening? Or just waiting to speak?**

Giving someone your full attention is called active listening. It is a process that involves:

1. **Concentrating** on what they are saying, which includes observing visual clues such as body language and also reading between the lines.
2. **Processing** the information you receive, and getting clarity by questioning and exploring where you are unsure.
3. **Choosing** how you wish to respond.

This is a very simple process, and yet much under-used.

What gets in the way of effective listening is:

- **Internal distractions** such as things on your mind, pressure you are under, stuff we are trying not forget, to do lists, worries, thinking ahead to later meetings, headaches, tiredness, thirst...

- **External distractions**, such as interruptions, ringing phones, email alerts, machinery, other conversations, the pile of paperwork on your desk, background music...

It makes you wonder how we ever manage to listen to each other at all!

Learning to be an active listener will help your one to one skills enormously. When a conversation is important, or it is a formal occasion such as a performance review, you will need this skill even more.

Things to think about

- **The environment.** If it is important, get away from the background noise and interruptions. Find a quiet appropriate place and turn your phone off.

- **Your head.** It may not come easily to clear the clutter from your brain, but do practice giving another person your full attention by stopping yourself deciding what to say next before they have finished speaking.

- **The timing**. Do think about the consequences of the time you choose. Have you allowed sufficient time to do the job properly? It is better to have some time left over than to run out.

- **Show a response** to what is being said. Eye contact, nodding, small facial expressions and the occasional repeating back of words and phrases all contribute to active listening.

The best aid to listening is genuine interest. If you really do want to know what the other person has to say, you will find it much easier to listen.

Summarising

Getting into the habit of summarising can reap rewards. By repeating back a short version of what you have heard, you give the other person the opportunity to correct you, as well as letting them know what you have taken on board and understood.

It is also a good tool for moving a discussion from one section to the next. A summary can work as a wrapping-up of one topic, freeing you up to move on to the next one.

It is the also a great way of forcing yourself to listen, if you know that every few minutes you will have to give a concise précis of what the other person has said.

Here's an example: *"So what you're telling me, John, is that the order would still be late going out even if I found you extra staff, because the packing machine is jammed. Is that right?"*

Questioning

In my opinion, effective questioning is one of the most significant skills gaps in managers today, yet it is a critical part of many workplace conversations.

Do you jump to conclusions?

Quite often on management training courses I give delegates a case study that asks them to get to the bottom of a problem situation by asking questions to find out what is going on.

So far, 70% of delegates or more have struggled to do this successfully.

Instead of exploring the issue, they go straight to finding a solution without being fully aware of what a problem actually is. They take information at face value, without challenging or investigating what is happening and what they have been told.

Needless to say, the actions and decisions they take are misguided to say the least!

To solve a problem effectively, or to get to the heart of the matter, it is important to ask the right questions. Sometimes it seems easier not to ask in case we open a can of worms. This is short-termism at its worst, akin to papering over the cracks, and will not stand us in good stead in the long run.

If you think you fully understand a situation it is still good policy to ask questions to clarify that you have the right end of the proverbial stick. Even if you learn nothing new other people involved will see that you have good understanding. This is likely to make them more cooperative and forthcoming, so you have nothing to lose.

One useful model to be aware of is called The Ladder of Inference (Senge) – it describes the thinking processes we go through in a nanosecond in any situation, and makes it easy to see how we get it wrong.

Here is a shamefully brief overview:

- **We pick up data.** So much is going on around us, we can't possibly take it all in so…

- **We filter the data and select what we notice.** *"The Boss looks serious today, he didn't even say good morning"*

- **We add meaning to the data, based on our experiences and beliefs of the world** *"It is so rude not to acknowledge staff. Common decency doesn't cost anything"*

- **We draw conclusions from the meaning we have added** *"He is rude. He is ignoring his staff. He doesn't know how to treat people. He takes us for granted"*

- **We make assumptions about how the world works** *"Bosses don't care about people. They are just in it for the money"*

- **We take action based on those assumptions.** *"I won't bother telling him we're all going out after work. He'd only spoil it"*

This happens in a moment all day long. Pity the poor Boss, who was so worried about his old Mum being taken into hospital last night that he lost concentration and had a bump in his car on the way in…

…he could really have done with that drink and a bit of support from the team!

Types of questions that work

Here is an overview of the types of questions you can use:

Open questions

These invite more than a one-word answer, and are used to get people talking. They usually start with:

What?

How?

Why?

Do be careful of using *"Why?"* questions. They have a habit of sounding parental and condemning. Would you rather be asked *"Why did you do that?"* Or *"what happened here?"*

If you have a situation to explore, prepare yourself by planning good questions in advance.

The same effect can be achieved by phrases used as questions, such as:

"Can you tell me about a time when ..."

"I wonder if you can think of an example of ..."

This approach is useful for job interviews and appraisals.

Probing

Sometimes an open question does not get you as much information as you would like. If this is the case, use a follow up question. This is called a probing question. In general, probing questions are used when you are seeking more detail or more understanding.

Don't be afraid to ask:

"What else?"

"What makes you say that?"

"What then?"

"What do you put that down to?"

"What influenced you?"

...and be prepared for both positive and negative information.

Closed questions

These invite one word or very brief answers. They often start with:

"Do you...?"

"Have you...?"

...which gets a yes/no type response, but you can also use what and when etc:

The replies are likely to be short, explicit and factual.

It is not true that open questions are the only 'good' questions. Closed questions can be a godsend when you need short sharp information, you need to move the pace on, or you are dealing with a rambler!

There are some good questioning strategies for specific circumstances in the remaining chapters of this book.

How not to question

Some styles of questioning are better avoided:

Leading questions

This is where you phrase the question in such a way as to suggest the answer. It's easily done; you assume the other person thinks same as you, and force them into a corner where it is hard for them to come out with the truth.

Also bear in mind that we find it much easier to say yes than no. You might also want to analyse the questions your boss asks you. Are you being taken in by leading questions?

Questions like these examples all make it difficult or the other person to be honest with you:

"You'd like to be on the project team wouldn't you?"

"Kevin is a slow worker, isn't he?"

"When are you reorganising the office?"

So, it's possible that you end up on the project team whether you like it or not, you feel guilty for bad mouthing Kevin when you think he's great, and now you feel obliged to reorganise the office when you had no plans to.

How could you reword these questions so that you get a more measured response?

Linking Questions

If you have planned ahead, you may well have a list of brilliant questions to take to your meeting. The danger here is that you come over something like an enthusiastic machine gun going full throttle.

There are two things to bear in mind here.

The first is to make sure the other person knows that you have heard and understood their answer before you launch into your next question.

The second thing is to link each of your questions to their last reply, so that it is more of a conversation and less of an interrogation. Links are likely to contain phrases such as:

"You were saying that..."

"Picking up on your thoughts, I was wondering..."

Multiple questions

If you bombard your colleague with multiple questions you are likely to confuse them – and yourself. Ask one question at a time.

Hypothetical Questions

The *"what if"* type of question can be very popular in some situations. However, what a person thinks they would do and what they actually do could be quite different.

You can use hypothetical questions to check out general feeling about options or test out assumptions you have made, but be wary of assuming that answers are fact.

The Three-Step Tango

Here is an assertiveness approach that makes good use of one very important truth: **Unless you understand where The Other Person Involved (Topi) is coming from, you are not really in a position to reach a conclusion about your own wishes or feelings, or to say what you want to happen.**

We often change our position when we realise what is really going on in a situation; far better to find out first rather than to have to back track later.

The 'Three-step Tango' uses both listening and questioning, and works in many situations. If you **Listen – Respond – Propose** in a conversation, you'll find yourself moving elegantly out of many a tricky situation:

1. **Listen until you understand where the other person is coming from.**

    Gather all the facts, feelings and circumstances. Try to get to the bottom of Topi's interests and motivation. Let him know you have heard and understood.

    •   Use listening and questioning techniques, such as open and probing questions

    •   Also use reflecting back and summarising to ensure you understand

    •   Maintain eye contact, use positive body language, such as nods and leaning slightly towards them

    •   Give your full attention

    •   Check your understanding so that there is no misinterpretation

    •   Acknowledge Topi's point of view

2. **Say what you think and feel about the situation**

    •   Describe how the situation has an impact on you

    •   Use appropriate language. Do not use *"but"*

    •   Be open, honest and straightforward

- Take responsibility for your feelings, using *"I"* rather than *"You make me..."*
- Assign your feelings/problem to behaviour or events – not the other person
- Remember to also allow Topi to express himself.

3. **Say what you would like to happen next, considering the consequences for yourself and the other person**

   - Be clear and specific about your needs - dropping hints or assuming may not work
   - Give Topi an opportunity to do the same
   - Be realistic. Define roles, time scales, etc
   - Do not get side tracked. Keep to the subject in hand
   - If the other person does not appear to have heard you, repeat the message
   - Be prepared to meet the other person half way. Offer a joint solution.

Body Language

We have already mentioned one very important thing you need to remember about body language:

If our words and body language contradict each other, it is always – **always** – our body language that will be believed.

Think about it. Imagine telling a friend that you can't make an event that is important to them. They say *"fine."* At the same time, they square their shoulders, and toss their hair and turn away from you. So, do you believe they are fine about it?

Body language supports what we say. We can't really work on what we say in isolation, we need to take body language into account.

Which of these could you try to help you assess how you are doing?

*   'Freeze frame' in different situations and note how you are holding yourself. Are you slumped, implying defeat and disinterest? Are you rigid with raised shoulders, indicating tension? Squared up, arms folded, as if you are looking for a fight? Hopefully, none of these things!

*   In your work clothes, sit or stand in front of a big mirror. Close your eyes, imagine yourself in different work situations. Think about what you say or do, don't open your eyes until you feel that your body is doing whatever it was in the real situation. Without moving, open your eyes, and have a good hard look at your body language. Think about how it might seem to others.

*   Call to mind a couple of people who seem to win respect everywhere they go. Also think of a person or two who never seem to be listened to or taken seriously. Next time you see them, observe their body language. Which are you more like? What can you learn from them?

It is also worth bearing in mind that our physical state has an impact on our mental state and mood. If you walk confidently with your head held high and a warm, friendly smile on your face, you will actually start to feel better about yourself. Others will be more at ease when they approach you, which in turn reinforces that you are a confident, friendly person...so you become one.

You may hear this called 'Behave to Become'. It is mentioned here because how we show ourselves to others does have an impact on our conversations. If this is an issue for you, there are other books that will explain it in more detail, for example Anthony Robbins' 'Unlimited Power'.

Sharing Respect

No doubt you want to be treated with courtesy and respect at work – we all like to feel that we are valued, which helps us to know that we are worthwhile human beings.

However, it's a fact that:

- respect can't be demanded; it has to be earned

- Topi also wants and deserves respect.

The good old principle of treating others how you would like to be treated yourself goes a long way towards addressing both of these points.

However, there is an underlying pitfall that undermines our face to face dealings with colleagues that nearly all of us fail to notice: our own distorted thinking. To be effective face to face you need to check what goes on inside your head, sometimes long and hard.

What does distorted thinking mean? It could be:

- Opinions and prejudices *"He's bound to be trouble if he comes from that side of town"*

- Jumping to conclusions *"She didn't say anything in the meeting. She must disapprove of my project"*

- Typecasting *"Looks like a hippy. Bound to be lazy"*

If you are to get the best out of your face to face conversations review your thoughts and feelings about the other person. They may have different beliefs and behaviours to you, more or less qualifications, be less talkative, more opinionated or flamboyant, but gaining respect means first giving it to people who work in different ways.

This doesn't mean abandoning your own personality, viewpoints and actions, but rather accepting and valuing the differences between you regardless of traits or status.

If your workplace has stringent rules about behaviour and dress that you can't go along with then you may be in the wrong job.

There will be situations where you will need to pull rank or have difficult conversations, but if you approach them from the viewpoint that the other person is a human being of equal worth and value but with a different role to play and different things to offer you are much more likely to have a positive outcome.

Challenging

The concept of challenging others often seems to scare people, as they see it as confrontational or squaring up for a fight. It really doesn't have to be like that.

Should we challenge?

First ask yourself if you have the right to challenge Topi, or if you're just being an interfering busybody. If the need to challenge is affecting your work or wellbeing, or it is your role to supervise Topi, you probably have a good case. If, though, you do not have Topi's respect, she is unlikely to listen to you.

You should also consider the consequences if you do not challenge when it is your place to do so. If you shy away from it you can damage your credibility, as it looks as if you are endorsing the behaviour by doing nothing. You are also denying Topi the opportunity to learn that there is a better way of behaving.

What and how do we challenge?

Many things are worth challenging when you come across them:

- Lack of realism or knowledge

- Distortion

- Assumptions

- Unreasonableness

- Failure to own a problem

- Evasions, game playing

- Failure to identify or understand consequences of behaviour

- Contradiction and inconsistent information

For this last instance 'The One to One Toolkit' (Reynolds and Cooper) suggests phrases like:

- *"I'm getting mixed messages from you. You say.... but do....."*

- *"On one hand..... but on the other hand..."*

- *"You tell me... but I see something different..."*

Whenever you identify behaviour that is unhelpful there are a number of techniques you can apply:

- **Giving feedback** *"Your tone of voice is very aggressive and loud right now. Are you aware of this?"*

- **Asking a direct question** *"Should you be asking Sam to do overtime at the weekends when you won't do it yourself?"*

- **Correcting and disagreeing** *"No, you are not stupid. You made one error, which is unlike you. That makes you human, not stupid"*

- **Invite Topi to change her language** – e.g. from *"I can't be in the same room as him"* to *"I choose not to be in the same room as him"*. This shift encourages Topi to be responsible for her own thoughts and actions.

- **Holding up a mirror** – helping Topi to see herself as others see her. *"Topi, how do you think it looks to others when you rush in at the last minute and then start eating your breakfast?"*

- **Giving silent attention** while Topi is busy erecting or maintaining her defences. This means that if Topi is coming up with poor excuses or reasoning, say nothing. She will probably become aware of what she is saying and realise that it doesn't sound good! If you can assist Topi to work out her own flaws, it will have much greater impact than you pointing them out will.

- **Calling her bluff** *"You say you're stupid? Ok, I'll arrange for you to be demoted...."* Hopefully this will lead to Topi correcting herself quickly!

- **Raising a moral agenda** *"Everyone has to start by learning. I think you are being unfair to the new apprentice..."*

- **Giving Topi the facts** *"Topi, this company's motto is Fast Service, Fair Prices. You kept the customer waiting for a week and then overcharged them."*

Always remember that if it's your job to manage then sometimes it's part of the job to manage difficult situations. In the long run you'll get no thanks for not grasping the nettle.

The key to challenging

The key, however, to challenging without seeming confrontational is remembering that body language and tone are believed over words. Make sure you eradicate any sign of disbelief or aggression, and replace it with the manner of an interested, concerned person who is curious. Challenging needs to be handled sensitively if you are not to lose Topi's trust.

Shutting People Up

In a book about conversations, we should acknowledge that there are times when we can't get a word in edgeways. Some folk make a habit of talking endlessly, because it is part of their personality to think out loud. Others do it to dominate, or fall into wittering when they are nervous.

Your first step in dealing with it is to think about the intent behind it. Is it just their personality, or are they acting this way to try to achieve something? This should give you a clue how to handle it.

You also need to think about how much of a problem it is. If it is a mild irritant to you, but a huge relief to Topi to get things off her chest, putting up with it might be your best approach; sometimes endurance is good for the soul.

If something needs to be done, here are some possible options:

- **Limit it** *"Topi, I have an urgent deadline, I only have five minutes..."*

- **Educate** *"You made a great point earlier, but it got lost because you spoke for so long. How about some training to help you learn to be more concise?"*

- **Send out non verbal signals** Look at your watch, drum your fingers, dart your eyes around the room...

- **Nod three times.** We nod when we agree, but if you do it three times, it indicates that you are ready to move on

- **Be direct.** Whether you do it at the time, or choose to bring it up later depends on the situation. *"Topi, I find it difficult that you talk so much. I think we could get as much done in our meeting in less time. Could you confine yourself to work topics?"*

The chapter on inappropriate behaviour might help if the problem is serious.

Saying No

Many of us find saying no difficult.

It goes against the grain – we think we are a nice person, and we want Topi to think that too. What will she think of us?

Common reasons for finding it hard to say no include:

- Not wanting others to think us unkind, uncooperative or selfish

- Wanting to be popular

- Thinking we should be all things to all people

- Thinking our refusal might cause offence or damage our career

- Having been brought up to think that saying "*No*" is impolite

- Finding it is easier to give in than risk the other person's reaction

- Not having a clear idea of our personal limits or boundaries

So, how do you say "No"?

- Practise saying no to small things.

- Rehearse out loud, too, as thinking through what we want to say is not as effective as actually speaking it out.

- Practise delivering your message in different ways, varying your words, pace and tone until you find the ways that suits you best. Don't forget to check your body language too.

- Get the word "*No*" out early in your response. If possible, make it the first word.

- Keep your response short - this gives less room for others to find a way in to try to persuade you to change your mind.

- Give reasons if you need to, but do not make excessive excuses. Usually people see through them.

- Do not apologise unnecessarily.

- Keep your non-verbal message assertive, and in harmony with your words. Maintain good eye contact and do not smile inappropriately.

- When you have finished making your point find a conversation closer such as *"OK?"* or *"Thank you for understanding"*, or just change the subject.

- If you are willing to do so, you can offer an alternative.

- Ask for time if you need it.

- Repeat yourself if necessary.

Remember you are turning down a request, not rejecting a person. You have a right to say *"No"*!

On the Hop

This book advises about preparing to have effective discussions, but that is not always possible.

We get stopped in the corridor, or find Topi in full flow next to us wanting a decision.

In this situation we tend to think that we are getting things done if we respond immediately, but what often happens is that we take things upon ourselves (*"leave it with me"*) that should be someone else's issue.

If you work in a quick response business you may need to make snap decisions, but it' a good approach to give yourself thinking time, even if it is only 10 minutes. You'd be surprised how often your first idea gets changed.

When you're caught on the hop:

- Firstly, and critically, decide if it is your issue to deal with or not. If not, signpost Topi in the right direction, even if it is back to her.

- Secondly, let Topi know that you have taken on board what she is saying. Acknowledging others' feelings, opinions and dilemmas does not imply that we agree, only that we have heard.

- Lastly, if it is your responsibility, consider how long you've got to reach an answer. Assure Topi that in order to make the right decision you will get back to her as soon as you have had time to think or get the information you need.

Remember not to be overly nice and take on work that should be Topi's. She will not grow and learn if you do it all for her. Perhaps you could help her to take more initiative or come up with some ideas before she brings problems to you.

You have probably also worked out that personality clashes come into play here. If Topi thrives on decisive action, and you tend to ruminate, you can imagine the consequences.

An awareness of you personal style is useful here too; some of us are programmed to get satisfaction from getting closure, i.e. taking action, even if it isn't the best thought out response. Others of us prefer to reflect for awhile, thinking through all possible options and gathering all relevant information before acting.

Warning!

Most of us never even consider the tone and pace of our speech, and yet so often it helps feed Topi's negative opinion of us.

If we speak quickly it can seem that we don't have time to listen. If we "*um*" and "*er*" a lot, we can sound as if we are unsure and unconfident. Neither may be true, but communication is hard enough without fuelling the fire of misunderstanding.

Common offenders are sounding:

- Abrupt

- Aggressive

- Patronising

- Sarcastic

- Distracted

...the list could go on, but you get the drift.

Listen to your voice, and ask yourself how it comes over.

When you've done that, ask others you trust for their opinion. Learning to change tone and pace is a small price to pay for immeasurably improving the success of your conversations.

3

Appraisals

Definition

An appraisal is a meeting between an employee and their Line Manager to review the employee's job performance over the past year. Usually it involves setting objectives for the coming year, and agreeing any training or development needs.

Some organisations call it a Performance Review, others call it a PDR (Personal Development Review).

Outcomes

The outcomes of the appraisal meeting include:

- The line manager has taken the opportunity to give feedback to the employee.

- Topi has a clear understanding of how she has progressed over the past year.

- Both parties benefit from stronger mutual understanding.

- An accurate record of the discussion is placed on the employee's personal file, including any objectives set and training needs identified.

Think Ahead

Before the appraisal meeting you need to prepare:

- **Forms.** Make sure in advance that you have the forms that need to be completed.

- **Job Description.** You will need to review a copy of the employee's job description, and check that they have a copy too.

- **Environment.** Make sure you arrange a suitable environment, i.e. a quiet, private office that is conducive to a productive, professional, discussion.

- **Time.** Make sure you allow plenty of time in your diary, not only for the meeting, but also for preparation beforehand and completing paperwork afterwards.

- **Evidence**. You will need real examples for evidence of performance. Ideally, you will have been collecting this throughout the year.

- **Rating system.** If you are using a rating system, make sure you are familiar with what the scales mean. Checking with others will help you make sure you are being consistent.

- **Objectives**. Give some thought to what appropriate objectives might be.

- **Issues.** Identify any specific issues that you want to discuss, e.g. praise, obstacles, career aspirations.

Steps

At the appraisal or performance review meeting:

- Set Topi at ease.

- Explain what is going to happen.

- Ask Topi how she thinks the previous year has gone. Confirm her views where you agree and note areas to discuss where your opinion differs.

- Share with Topi your views of her performance, supported by evidence and examples.

- Have a discussion around Topi's aspirations, interests and obstacles to progress.

- Discuss and set realistic and relevant objectives.

- Identify and agree relevant learning and development needs.

- Ask if there is anything else Topi wishes to discuss.

- Complete all forms.

- Tell Topi what happens next.

Good Practice

Appraisals, or performance reviews, are important meetings so they deserve sufficient planning and preparation.

They are part of a year long cycle, not a stand-alone event, so should be viewed in this context.

A typical annual cycle looks like this:

- **Appraisal meeting.** Work performance is reviewed with the line manager. Objectives are set and development needs identified.

- **Support.** The line manager offers support and feedback as the employee works towards their goals throughout the year.

- **Review.** Typically there will be one or two meetings during the year to monitor progress. This is an opportunity to check that the goals set are still relevant, and to identify any unforeseen obstacles that may have sprung up.

- **Performance.** The employee uses and hones new skills while the manager notes improvements and setbacks, continuing to support.

- **Self-assessment.** Towards the end of the yearly cycle, employees are given the opportunity to reflect on their performance using their current job description as a guide.

- ....and then back to appraisal.

Paperwork

Most companies will have an appraisal process in place already. Usually, the forms are issued to the employee a couple of weeks before the meeting to give them the opportunity to write their own comments about how they think they have performed, using their job description as a guide.

If you work for small company that has nothing in place, be sure to allow yourself time to come up with a system that suits you and is fit for purpose.

If you have existing forms to use, do not let them dictate to you. The quality of the conversation is much more important than the order you fill the form in. Step back and think carefully about what it is you want to achieve. Then, take a look at the form with fresh eyes and consider how well it will help you achieve your aims.

There is no law that says you have to start at beginning and work through to the end. Think objectively about the order you complete the form in. For example, some forms begin with a long list of attributes to score the employee against. This can be demotivating for the individual concerned, and may not necessarily work in favour of creating the right environment.

Also make sure that the forms are sent to Topi with enough time for her to reflect and complete the paperwork. It is probably worth touching base with her before the meeting to make sure she has completed the form to save you wasting your time; also you can offer help if she is struggling with it.

The environment

Don't underestimate the importance of the environment. Getting the location right for the meeting will considerably increase your chances of success. Getting it wrong could seriously devalue it in Topi's eyes. Don't use a busy workplace where you cannot control interruptions and distractions. It should be:

- **Private.** Even a meeting in an office with a glass wall is not ideal.

- **Quiet.** Background noise will distract the flow of conversation and thoughts.

- **Professional** but comfortable. Sitting either side of a desk can psychologically suggest opposition. Can you come up with a better arrangement? At right angles can work well.

- **Relaxed** – but not too much so. You are aiming for professional yet approachable, so that Topi feels she can talk freely.

Starting the meeting

So, assuming that the paperwork is in place, let's turn our attention to the actual appraisal meeting. We have already said that you may need to start by setting Topi at ease; she may be nervous and expecting the worst. Explain to her what is going to happen, what will be recorded, and how long the meeting will take.

Once the scene is set, you can move on to the heart of the matter. Bear in mind that you are aiming for a constructive dialogue, and not a monologue from you. Try to make sure that Topi speaks at least 50% of the time. 70% would be even better. Also remember that all points are much better made if you can get Topi to reach a conclusion by you questioning her rather than telling her.

When you ask Topi how she thinks the previous year has gone, be sure to explore her answers to make sure you understand her point of view. Link her answers to the job description, and let her know when you agree with her assessment. If there is a gap between her view of her performance and yours, you will need to decide whether to tackle it there and then or wait for her to finish her review, and return to it when you begin yours. Ideally, the two can be woven together.

When you are explaining your views, support them with evidence using specific examples.

Here is a simple framework you can use to give structure to your discussion. For each topic:

- **Introduce** the topic and use an open question to get conversation started, such as *"How have you found...?"*.

- **Develop** the topic by listening, exploring and using probing questions.

- **Consolidate** by adding your observations, thoughts and feedback, and agreeing common ground.

- **Conclude** by paraphrasing to check that you have a shared understanding. This effectively shuts down each topic so that you can move on to the next one.

Overlooking talent?

A common mistake that managers make is to pigeon hole staff, assuming that they're only capable of doing what they've always done. This short-sightedness can lead to talent being overlooked and potential not being recognised. When you have a discussion around Topi's aspirations, be sure to include things like of her work interests, willingness to train, what she thinks her obstacles to progress may be, and any other issue pertinent to her job performance and future employment. This conversation is likely to digress from the job description, but could prove invaluable in the future. Understanding career goals can often give clues that will help you understand her motivation.

Let Topi know that you have heard what she says, even if she raises issues you cannot act on right now. You will be able to stay on track better if you say that you will pick up concerns that are outside the scope of the appraisal meeting at another time.

Setting objectives

There are two different types of goals or objectives that come out of an appraisal meeting. They are

- objectives around work performance, such as targets and projects, and also

- learning and development objectives.

You have probably already heard the objectives should be SMART – specific, measurable, achievable, relevant and time bound. This is a good start, but far from the end of the story. Of course, objectives need to be linked to improving job performance, but they should also be motivating. If the individual concerned is not really convinced by the objective, they are not likely to approach it with gusto.

You may be responsible for making sure that Topi has objectives, but they do not all need to be your ideas. You will get much better buy in if suggestions come from Topi. Try to incorporate at least some of her thoughts or wording into the final objectives. This will make it easier for Topi to identify with them and take ownership.

Another important factor that helps is that the objectives should be sufficiently stretching. If they are too simple they will fail to inspire, while if they are too challenging you could be setting Topi up to fail. What is Topi's view? Make sure you check that she thinks they are do-able, and ask what support or resources she thinks she will need.

Quantity is also important. Between four and six objectives is about average, but use common sense. If one of them is a large project, think of the over all workload and adjust accordingly; ditto if several of them can be quickly and easily achieved.

Development needs

Do go into the meeting with some ideas for suitable development opportunities for Topi. As with objectives, it is preferable if Topi has her own thoughts and suggestions. Sometimes people find it hard to identify learning or development needs; often they cannot see further than the in house list of training courses.

There are hundreds of ways of helping a person learn a skill or grow in knowledge. Once you have identified areas where it would be useful for Topi to develop, try to be creative about how these needs are met. Undoubtedly budget is limited, and training courses are not the answer to everything.

Also take into consideration Topi's learning style, and her current level of competence. Choose ways of learning that they will enjoy engaging in as far as possible.

One danger here is that sometimes a team member can be very enthusiastic about learning, identifying legions of training courses that they would like to attend. You will need to prioritise according to the demands of the job, which may mean that they cannot have all their wishes. You will need to explain this to Topi, while commending her keenness.

Development activity is usually collated into a training plan, which lists the learning objectives, deadlines, and methods of achieving them.

Ending the meeting

Do give Topi the opportunity to raise any issues or ask questions at the end of the appraisal.

Also ask her for some immediate feedback on how she found the meeting – this will help you know if your own aims have been met.

Make sure that all forms are filled in and signed. Tell Topi what happens next, for example when objectives will be reviewed and what the next steps are for putting the training plan into action.

If you are the appraisee ...

Of course, you might be the appraisee. This is a really important meeting for you, as it is your chance to show self awareness and highlight your aspirations.

From reading the above, you can probably deduce the preparation you need to do before your appraisal meeting. Make sure your job description is up to date, assess your performance against every point on it.

Do not assume that your manager has noticed all the good things you have done – unfortunately, the mistakes are more likely to stick in his mind! Plan to ensure that your boss has a full understanding of your skills, experience and achievements.

Also think about what learning and development will help you progress. Do some research into the best ways of learning the skills you want to acquire, with options if possible. You will need to put a good business case forward for any requests, so be prepared to say how the organisation will benefit from investing in you.

Finally, be prepared to take an active part in the discussion - your boss will thank you for it!

Warning!

Appraisal is NOT...

- a disciplinary meeting. There are other, separate processes for addressing serious issues to do with a job holder's conduct or capability, which should be followed and used; see the chapters on Disciplinary Meetings and Performance Gaps

- a discussion you 'save things up for'. Whether it is praise or criticism, feedback is only effective if given at the time, or as soon as possible. There should be **no surprises** in the appraisal discussion, but rather a review of previous feedback and discussions throughout the year.

- Just a review of past performance. There is little point in simply looking backwards.

- A time to be vague. Be explicit and concise in all areas, supporting your thoughts with real examples and evidence.

4

Challenging Attitude and Negativity

Definition

An intervention where you are seeking to persuade a colleague to change their unhelpful or negative attitude.

This is not about their work performance – what they do – it could be about moaning or being grumpy; how they communicate and behave with colleagues.

Outcomes

- Topi is aware of the impact of her behaviour on colleagues and workflow.

- Topi is aware of what acceptable attitude and behaviour looks and sounds like.

And hopefully -

- Topi knows how to change her behaviour and find appropriate support.

- Agreement is reached on a way forward that is acceptable to all sides.

Think Ahead

- What is the intent behind the behaviour? Are you making an assumption?

- What will be different if the behaviour is changed?

- What will happen if the behaviour remains the same?

- Will the rewards of the behaviour change outweigh the effort of tackling the situation?

- Do you have concrete, first hand examples of the behaviour in question?

- Do you have an accurate understanding of the impact of the behaviour on others?

- Are you able to describe the preferred behaviour in a way that will be understood?

- What are the boundaries of acceptable behaviour in your workplace? Is this documented anywhere?

Steps

Nipping it in the bud:

- Identify the behaviour

- Say what it means to you

- Ask for confirmation

- Describe more helpful behaviour if you need to

Longer term:

- Create a calm, supportive environment.

- Reiterate Topi's strengths, and her value to the organisation.

- Raise the issue of concern, describing acceptable boundaries in the workplace and the impact of her current behaviour. Be clear and unambiguous.

- Ask Topi to tell you how she would like things to be at work.

- Ask Topi what behaviour would help her achieve her aims.

- Describe what better attitude or behaviour would be like. Be as specific as you can.

- Ask them how this could be achieved and offer support.

Good Practice

Should you challenge?

If someone is doing their job adequately, challenging them about attitude or negative behaviour can feel like skating on thin ice. After all, should we even bother if their output is acceptable?

You'll also be aware that there's a perception that challenging someone has to be confrontational or argumentative.

We also believe that attitude can be the hardest thing to change. This means that we are often reluctant to challenge, hoping instead that things will get better somehow. Meanwhile, if the rest of the team are catching the negative vibes and getting fed up you'll feel that something needs to be done, before you find you've lost half a dozen great workers for the sake of keeping one mediocre one.

Often we try dropping hints or getting tetchy with Topi, hoping he will work out the reason for our displeasure for himself. Maybe that will work, but more likely it won't.

The good news!

The reality is that quite often attitude can be changed, with sane, rational adults at least. Sometimes the worst offenders have no idea of the impact on their team-mates, and once they discover that they are upsetting other people they like or respect they can't wait to do things differently.

It won't be a stand off if you have prepared and thought through what it is you want to achieve. Your aim is to be assertive, but also sensitive to Topi's feelings.

Ignoring the signs

One of the problems here is that the behaviour connected to attitude can be hard to nail down, as it is often about tone and body language rather than the actual words spoken (e.g. eyes rolling, huffing and puffing, tutting, sighing, abruptness).

We often tend to ignore these things, even when they contradict the words being spoken (e.g. *"I'm fine! I can cope!"*) the longer it goes on, the harder it becomes to address it.

Why do they do it?

Think for a moment about why so many people act in a way that is irritating or demotivating to others. Behaviour is learned, and then becomes habit.

Often they are not even aware of what they are doing – or how it is interpreted. If they have some awareness, but no one (including you) has ever asked them to change, the message they have received by default is that their behaviour is acceptable.

Also be aware that there must be some pay off for them – what might it be?

- They get to stay in their comfort zone. Habits and ritual behaviour can make us feel safe. Comfort zones always have some appeal, even they are filled with rubbish.

- It saves them the bother of having to think about changing. A big concern with change is that we won't be able to cope, or it will expose our weaknesses.

- They know they are welcome at the pity party. It's one way of getting attention, isn't it?

Making it stop

Many people who make an art form of being negative get away with it because no one takes them to task. Here is a simple technique you can use when confronted with non-verbal huffiness. It is a remarkably effective technique; it works because it brings out into the open behaviours that we often choose to ignore. The stages are:

1. Identify the behaviour

2. Say what it means to you

3. Ask for confirmation

For example, you might say: *"(1) Emma, every time I mention the project deadline, you sigh and roll your eyes. (2) I take it this means you have a problem with the dates. (3) Am I right?"*

Or *"(1) John, I've noticed that whenever we discuss the new product launch, you shake your head and look at your feet. (2) To me, it looks like you disapprove of something. (3) Am I correct? Can we talk about this?"*

Think how these conversations might progress. Emma and John either have to agree with your perception, or deny that their actions have been interpreted accurately – in which case you can have a conversation about their true feelings and why they are using behaviour that contradicts what they are telling you.

In reality, what usually happens is that the person is surprised to be approached, sometimes denies the interpretation – and is then often quick to stop the behaviour.

Replacing behaviour

If we ask someone to stop behaving in a certain way, we have only done half of the job.

Never assume that the person knows what to replace the unwanted behaviour with.

We all have a repertoire of learned behaviour, which may or may not include something suitable we can use to replace the unwanted conduct. To be clear in our mission, we need to be able to explain, coach or describe what is needed instead.

As with most one to one interventions, the ideal way forward would be to help the person work it out for themselves if it all possible.

Entrenched behaviour

When behaviour is more deep-rooted, you can use a similar process to the three stage technique outlined above, but more time and care is needed.

For a start, a challenge about how one behaves can be quite a shock. You may need to allow time for an emotional response to be worked through.

To begin, make sure Topi understands that you value his strengths and worth to the organisation. This isn't so much about sugaring the pill as keeping the conversation in context. People are prone to extremes when challenged, and may catastrophise, imagining things are far worse than they actually are. Help him keep a sense of proportion.

Remember that you are taking issue with certain behaviours, not the whole person.

But!

If you have a criticism to make, don't use *"but…"*!

"But…" somehow manages to delete everything that has gone before it.

Instead, just use the 'Full stop. New sentence' approach.

So, instead of, *"Bill, you're one of our fastest workers, but there is something I'd like to discuss…"* try *"Bill, you're one of our fastest workers. I have something I'd like to discuss…"*

The difference is that the compliment is not devalued, which puts the other person in a better position for dealing with the criticism.

Next describe accurately the behaviour or attitude that is unhelpful. Use real examples rather than sweeping generalisations. Be aware of pace, allow Topi time to digest what you are saying, even pausing in silence. Explain the impact on the work environment. Be very aware of your manner.

John Heron sets the scene well when he says 'Tell the truth without compromise and with love'. You might prefer to use the word 'respect' instead of 'love', but the essence remains.

Ask Topi how he would like things to be (*How would you like your colleagues to view you? How would you like to respond to others? What would you like to achieve at work?*), then ask what type of behaviour would help her reach her ideal scenario.

You may need to be patient and persist here. If he doesn't see the need to change, it's never going to happen.

Depending on the experience and maturity of the person, this may be easy or completely alien to them – they may have no idea how to behave differently. Some people (really!) at this point have a light switched on, realise they have a choice and immediately begin behaving in a better way. For others, it may be down to you to explain exactly what they need to do to behave acceptably. New behaviour can be difficult to learn (old dog, new tricks...), and ingrained habits are even harder to break. You will need to understand this and be supportive.

Depending on how it goes, you may choose to be blunt on the possible outcomes if the behaviour does not change. If the penny has dropped, however, don't use a sledgehammer.

Do

- Think what it is like to be in their shoes.

- Think through what you are asking - what will be required of them to change their behaviour? What are the actual steps they will need to take?

- Do allow space and silence.

- Do persist.

Don't

- Don't tackle the issue while your emotion is running high.

- Don't expect a personality transplant.

- Don't pussyfoot. Or clobber.

Warning!

- Resist the temptation to get it over with as quickly as possible. Yes, it's not easy to challenge, but going at it like a steam train won't help at all.

- There are two sides to every story. Make sure you have first hand information. If it is all second hand, do not challenge. Investigate and explore instead until you have the evidence you need.

- If someone who has always been a ray of sunshine begins behaving badly there is probably a cause, which may or may not be work related.

5

Introducing Change

Definition

A discussion where a colleague is informed of a change that is coming that will affect their work or environment.

Outcomes

- You will have explained clearly and explicitly the need for the change, including details such as timescales, and how it will impact on Topi.

- You will have effectively dealt with Topi's initial concerns and questions.

- Topi will understand how the changes will affect her and what she needs to do differently.

Think Ahead

- How will the change benefit Topi? Or inconvenience her?

- Why is the change necessary?

- How will you get buy in?

- Is she already aware that the change is needed? How much of a shock will it be?

- What will Topi need to give up or let go of?

- Is Topi equipped to make the change, or will she need support?

- How is she likely to respond?

- Can you describe the future scenario in a way that Topi can identify with?

Steps

- **Explain to Topi** why the status quo needs to change.

- **Lead Topi briefly through the process** leading to the decision to make the change. Keep it brief and relevant to her.

- **Describe what the future scenario will be like** as fully as possible.

- **Allow Topi to express her feelings** about the situation.

- **Describe the steps and timescales** that will take place to make the change happen.

- **Check that Topi understands**, address any initial concerns.

Good Practice

People react to change in many different ways. Even positive changes can meet a wall of resistance and emotion. This should not come as a surprise, yet often it does. A quick look back at personality traits in The Basics, or learning styles in the chapter on coaching, will show how people vary in their reactions and preferred ways of behaving.

With this wide range, little wonder that introducing change needs planning. Focusing on the needs of the people involved is central to success, but often gets neglected, leaving them floundering.

Change has an impact...

Think, for a moment, about your comfort zone.

Take, for example, using your own kitchen.

You know where to find everything you need, the quirks of your oven and where the plug points are. Making tea and toast is as easy, little thought required. You can probably keep an eye on the news and hold a conversation at the same time.

Now, imagine that you have been transported to a brand new, state of the art kitchen, containing the very best of everything. Big glossy, shiny surfaces abound, all appliances look like modern art. Now go make your toast and tea.

How do you feel? For a start, you need more concentration, because you have to make a conscious effort to find the things you need. It might take longer while you work out how the new fangled kettle works. You might burn your toast, because it's your first attempt at using unfamiliar equipment.

In a nutshell, that warm, comfortable, safe feeling we have when we are in our comfort zone is absent.

This is why Topi might resist the change, even if it is beneficial to her in the long run; the current situation may not be ideal, but it is her comfortable reality.

In addition, if we are asked to do something differently we can begin to doubt our competence because suddenly we feel as if we are wearing L plates again. Often, this is coupled with nagging doubts – what if we can't make the changes? Will we be seen as slow or unskilled? Will everyone else get to grips with it faster than you, leaving you behind? Confidence levels start to go downhill.

Sometimes our irrational inner child brings tantrums to the fore: *"I don't want to! I like my life just the way it is!"*

In summary, change is a challenge to our...

- Comfort

- Competence

- Confidence

- Control

...so we resist it!

The Change Curve

With any change a loss of some kind is involved, so it follows that a form of mourning is natural in many cases.

Loss and mourning follow a change curve: the stages that we go through when faced with change. This is based on Elisabeth Kübler Ross's original work based on observing the bereaved, but other researchers have found that the model holds true for most changes in life, and many have interpreted it in a business context.

Some stages you might see Topi go through are

- **Shock or surprise** *" It can't be true!" "It's not happening!"*

- **Denial** Displaying ostrich tendencies. *"...if I stick my head in the sand and ignore it, it will go away and I can carry on the way I have always done"*

- **Anger** and frustration *"Why me? It's not fair!"*

- **Depression** and apathy - feelings of being helpless, lack of self confidence, not being able to see a way forward. *"I'll look stupid if I can't get the hang of it...."*

- **Looking for a way forward** to bring ourselves out of the depression and apathy. *" I suppose I could try..."*

- **Accepting** and deciding how to implement the change - beginning to see a way through it. *"I'll give it three months..."*

- **Integrating** the change into your work or life.

(Adapted from Cooper and Reynolds in The One to One Toolkit)

Depending on her personality, Topi may get stuck at some point in the curve, and need more support to get through.

Here's how to address some of the more common sticking points:

Denial

Shock and denial are at the beginning of the change curve. You may find that some people behave like ostriches – they put their head in the sand, and fully intend to keep it there, believing that the change will go away if they ignore it long enough. They know that change leads to uncertainty and insecurity, so is best avoided. Denial protects you from having to deal with change – and you can't fail if you don't try, can you?

It is easy to overlook Topi when she is in denial, because she may seem to be going about her business as usual and it may not be apparent at first. She may avoid you, or withdraw at any opportunity.

Dealing with denial:

- Make the unknown known as far as possible, so that Topi can visualise the future and her place in it.

- Offer reassurance. Be gentle but firm. Often, just understanding the stages of the change curve can be enough to help Topi see that what she is experiencing is a normal part of adapting to change.

- Acknowledge Topi's feelings. Often we feel we are not heard when we have no control over events. You may not be able to stall the change, but you can let Topi know she has been heard. Do not underestimate the value of this.

- Make it ok to fail. Expecting everyone to get it right every time when you asking them to do something differently is unrealistic.

Resistance

This is the stage that involves anger and depression. People are letting you know that they are not happy, blaming and complaining at any opportunity. You may see outbursts of temper, or passive/aggressive behaviour.

They may feel that because they are being asked to do things differently it implies that what they have been doing until now is worthless. They also believe the old way works perfectly well, and they resent things being imposed in them.

Dealing with resistance:

- Acknowledge their frustration.

- Make it very transparent why the status quo has to change – while recognising their contribution.

- Limit their destructiveness - let them rip with you...

- ...But be assertive when it comes to letting them know how damaging their negativity is to others.

Exploration

When people reach this stage, they have accepted the change and are looking for ways to make it happen. They may experiment with different approaches, or have lots of ideas – and some will be better than others. At this point, you need to watch out for the impulsive types. They may jump into quickly, volunteering to take the lead, acting before all the facts are known, or capitalising on the chance to raise their profile.

To get the best out of Topi at this stage:

•   Harness her enthusiasm, and praise her for it.

•   Recognise that she gets satisfaction from completing a task, not the process, so try to find smaller steps that she will find rewarding.

•   Give her all the facts and make sure she takes them into account.

•   Emphasise timescales – there is no reward for early completion!

•   Increase supervision, so that you can channel Topi's enthusiasm and prevent her going off at a tangent.

Communicate, communicate, communicate!

By now, you will have realised that communicating change requires you to be on the ball constantly, making more time than usual to deal with Topi and make sure she is coping. To get the commitment you should be more accessible and visible than normal, to offer reassurance, deal with issues, and to make the future scenario a reality.

•   Know the compelling reason you are asking your people to work, think and interact differently.

•   Be able to articulate it, using language Topi understands and identifies with.

•   Have a clear idea of the desired state as far as possible. Be able to describe it as fully as possible – hard and soft factors.

•   Communicate effectively, consistently, repeatedly using a variety of methods to back up your conversations. If you let up, Topi will revert to old behaviours.

- Break it down into steps so that she can see progress on the journey.

- Make sure Topi is not isolated. Find activities that create involvement, sharing ideas and working together.

Even after all of this she'll still think there's something you're not telling her!

Warning!

- People have a capacity to forget things they don't want to hear. You may need a series of conversations, not just one, to convince Topi that the change is not going to go away.

- Don't take the anger or upset personally. Familiarise yourself with the change curve so that you recognise the stages your people are going through. Just don't expect them to go through the stages at the same pace, or in the same way.

6

Coaching

Definition

Enabling another person to improve their performance by helping them to learn rather than teaching them.

This means using a range of skills to give them support to reach their goals.

Outcomes

- Topi's skills, knowledge or attitude are improved, leading to increased productivity.

- Topi is more self aware and prepared to take responsibility for his own actions.

- Topi's willingness to solve problems and be self motivated increases.

Think Ahead

- You will need to recognise opportunities to hold coaching conversations.

- Who could you coach?

- When would be a good time?

- What exactly is it you hope to achieve by coaching Topi?

- Prepare in advance a good list of coaching questions you can use.

- Think what might be suitable goals to set at the end of the coaching session.

Steps

- **Define the current situation** – what is going on right now?

- **Establish the desired situation**/skillset/behaviour – this is the goal.

- **Explore options** for getting to the desired situation, and help Topi to choose the best one.

- **Discuss any potential obstacles** with Topi, and work with him to come up with strategies for dealing with them.

- **Plan the steps** needed to turn the chosen option into a workable path to the goal.

Good Practice

Coaching is very much flavour of the month at the moment, almost everybody seems to be a coach or have one. There is a slight issue here in that there isn't really one recognised definition of coaching.

What type of coaching?

At one end of the scale is simply passing on work based skills through short, opportunistic conversations.

At the other is much deeper and more complex work involving several prearranged sessions, helping individuals find direction and challenging them to come up with their own solutions.

This latter approach requires an advanced skills set which is usually acquired through a substantial training course that involves practice, observation and supervision. It is a specialist role, so here we are concentrating on the type of coaching that happens by spotting an opportunity and taking advantage of it.

What makes a coaching conversation?

In most workplaces there are everyday occasions where you can have a coaching conversation that helps someone move forward. For example, you could consider coaching when:

- New procedures need putting in place.

- You're delegating new or different work.

- A change is being implemented.

- You want to prepare someone to take more responsibility or promotion.

- There is an incident that can be learned from.

- Topi has been successful, and you want to help him identify why it went so well, so that he can repeat the behaviour

How adults learn

Having spotted an opportunity or two, what next? Some of knowledge about how adults learn and develop would be useful.

Firstly, be aware of the learning cycle. When something happens, we only learn from it if we:

- Reflect on it – What happened?
- Draw conclusions – So what?
- Decide what we would like to differently in the future – What next?
- Put into practice our new plan

Then something will happen, and the cycle starts again (this is adapted from Kolb).

When you are coaching, it can be quite straightforward to think of a line of enquiry and questions that will help Topi reflect, conclude and plan.

There are some aspects to learning you may not have realised:

- We tend to be more problem centred than subject centred. This means that you need to give Topi a target that makes sense to him, where he can see it addresses his needs. He will be most motivated and engaged if the learning relates to goals that he has set himself.
- Topi will learn best when he doesn't just memorise information or instructions. It's understanding that leads to retention, not memory. Try the EDIP (explain, demonstrate, imitate, practise) approach to take Topi from unaware to proficient. Reinforcement like this is necessary to transfer learning into long term memory. Without reinforcement the short term memory will let new learning go.

- Topi will learn most effectively through activity that takes place at his own pace, with material that seems relevant.

- When using examples, make the link between the new learning and Topi's previous experience or knowledge.

- Feedback should be built in to learning, or Topi will not know when he has learnt successfully.

- Learning is more successful when you move from simple processes in stages to more complex ones.

- Short bursts of learning are more effective than continuous learning, so breaking new material into manageable units is a good approach.

Learning styles

We have different learning styles so you may need to be flexible, both in your approach and the way you help Topi set action points. There are several theories about learning styles, but Honey and Mumford's is one of the most popular.

They identified four different learning styles. Most of us use several of them, but some people have a clear preference for only one. This helps us understand what type of activity we will learn most easily from.

Learn to recognise Topi's learning style, and adapt your approach to suit him. Here is a brief description of the styles with tips on how to tackle them.

Activists

Activists are happiest when immersed in something new. They tend to be gregarious, and love brainstorming. Because they are motivated by new challenges, they can get bored with implementation and seeing things through. You are unlikely to find them passively sitting in the corner, as they will be off seeking their next adventure. Sitting and listening to a lecture is their idea of torture!

To help an activist learn:

- Give him the limelight, i.e. ask him to chair meetings, lead discussions, give presentations.

- Involve him with other people to bounce ideas off them, solving problems as part of a team.

- Make it 'here and now' activity so he can see immediate relevance.

- Give him short and sharp bursts of learning.

- Make it fun.

- Throw him at the deep end and let him work it out for himself!

Reflectors

Reflectors need time to think things through. They like to sit back and observe, considering the situation for all directions. They collect data from different sources and weigh it up thoughtfully before reaching conclusions. They are by nature cautious and may take a back seat, but they will enjoy watching and listening to others, as it is part of their information gathering.

Theorists like to learn at their own pace. If you force them to react immediately, or jump in at the deep end, they will not be best pleased.

To help a reflector learn:

- Tell him what to expect and give him time to prepare before the learning session.

- Let him learn at his own pace.

- Give him time to think things over or do more research. He likes depth of knowledge.

- Let him have the full picture and see the future implications.

Theorists

Theorists like to think through an issue in a logical, rational way. They will integrate new information into theories they already know, or form new ones, which comes naturally to them.

They will find patterns and links between pieces of information. They approve of models, principles and systems thinking. They are perfectionists who work step by step, looking for sense and meaning. They can be detached and dedicated to objectivity.

They are not keen on ambiguity or subjectivity. Anything flippant or whacky will make them distinctly uncomfortable. They will also be frustrated if they cannot research in depth.

To help a theorist learn:

- Give them the ideas or concept behind the learning.

- Structure the learning and present it in a logical order.

- Make it possible for them to be precise and methodical.

- Give them clear objectives.

Pragmatists

Pragmatists, like activists, like to try out new ideas, but the difference is that the ideas need to have relevance to them. They are keen to bring new learning to the workplace, and will quickly get on with new ways of working if they can see the benefit it will bring.

They are practical, down to earth types who may have little patience with the theorists and reflectors, preferring to get on with things rather than talk or think about them. They are fast workers, confident who like to find practical solutions to problems. They like a challenge as long as it links to their world.

To help a pragmatist learn:

- Make it practical and applicable.

- Keep it focused – don't waste their time.

- Let them try out the learning as soon as possible.

- Emphasise the relevance to their role.

Why should you get this right?

If Topi has to learn in a style that he is not comfortable with, he may need more time, or extra support; he may even lose motivation.

You can find out Topi's learning style if he completes a questionnaire. There are several versions available online. Observing Topi at work may help you work out his, too.

Some thought and preparation up front on your part can make coaching someone else much more effective and rewarding.

Coaching questions

The key to successful coaching is to have a good repertoire of questions. There are many easily accessible lists online. Here is a sample of the types of questions that are useful:

"What's important to you?"

"What is the problem in a nutshell?"

"What have you done so far to improve things?" "What else could you try?"

"What is standing in your way?" "How could you overcome it?"

"What is the best use of your time?"

"What will be different when you have achieved your goal?"

"What will happen if you don't achieve this goal?"

"What is the worst thing / the best thing that could happen?"

"How will it feel to do that?"

"What can you control?" "What is outside your control?"

"What is stopping you from doing it right now?"

"What can you learn from that?"

"Who could help you?"

"What will make the biggest difference?"

"Do you have a gut feeling about this?"

"Have you solved problems like this before?"

"What would you advise yourself?"

There are many books on coaching you could read. If you manage a team, it would be wise to study further. Two of the most popular authors are:

- Tim Gallwey, who is most famous for writing The Inner Game series, and

- John Whitmore who wrote Coaching for Performance.

John Whitmore's GROW model is probably the best known and most widely used. A brief overview follows, but do be aware that there are many other similar models around.

The GROW model of coaching

There are four stages to GROW:

Goals What does Topi want to achieve? What are his aspirations?

Reality What is the current situation? Can you describe it an accurate, precise way?

Options What options are there? How many different ways are there of moving forward? What are the pros and cons of each? Which is the best choice?

Will Action Planning. What is Topi going to do as a result of the coaching? What steps will he take?

Let's have a further look at these stages:

Goals

Whitmore's model begins by exploring what it is that Topi wants to achieve. The coach's job here is to help Topi be realistic, focussed and clear. The much-used SMART acronym can help – but don't forget the BMW! You'll know that goals are often set because Topi thinks it is something he half-heartedly thinks he should do, or he feels his boss wants him to do. What does Topi really want? If you can't see signs of enthusiasm or commitment, you probably haven't got it cracked.

A goal will succeed if it is **A SMART BMW**

- Specific
- Measurable
- Achievable
- Relevant
- Time bound
- BMW- But Must Want i.e. something you really want to do

It should also be:

- Broken down into manageable steps
- Focused on performance, rather than extrinsic factors

One approach that can help is to ask *"On a scale of 1-10, how committed are you to this goal?"*, followed up by some discussion around *"What would it take for you to turn that into a 10?"* It will soon become apparent whether or not Topi is really convinced by the goal.

You can see that it may be risky to take goals Topi suggests at face value. Always be curious, explore, and challenge to find out if the goal is sound.

Reality

Understanding the reality will give you a context to work with, and also help you understand both the challenges Topi faces, and also the opportunities he has to maximise. To clarify the current situation you will use skills like exploring, probing, and summarising. Generalisations will not do. You need a sharp, specific focus.

- Remain objective. It is easy to get reality distorted by expectations, hopes and fears, prejudices etc. To help you not get drawn in, stay detached and ask questions that require factual responses. You can also encourage Topi to describe what the situation is, rather than giving you his opinions or assumptions.

- You may need to help Topi increase his self awareness, or become more deeply aware of factors that can influence his success. Try and follow his train of thought.

- Take note of body language. This may give you clues about his confidence, fears, or attitude.

- This is coaching, not psychotherapy. If you unveil issues that you are not comfortable discussing you should not stray out of your area of competence. Instead, refer Topi on to someone who can help.

Options

Generating options helps to give Topi ownership of the process. The best approach is to ask him for his ideas first, prompting if necessary. Topi is more likely than you are to come up with options that are viable, and suit his learning or behavioural style. Only pitch in with your suggestions when you are sure that Topi has run dry with his own ideas.

If Topi can be helped to weigh up the options and identify which suits his needs best, he is much more likely to be committed to succeeding. It also gets the brain into gear and can be very motivating.

- You will need to be able to judge when enough options have been produced. If you have too many, weighing them up becomes a very long job! Be influenced by the importance of the topic at hand. A trivial issue does not merit hours of option generating, but more time and thought should be given for the big issues.

- Help Topi to come up with ideas that may not naturally occur to him. Techniques like brainstorming and mind mapping can help here. You may need to suspend your own desire for closure, or be aware when Topi wants to move on.

- You may need to deal with negative assumptions (*"That won't work", " it can't be done", "it will take too much time"*) You could ask '*What if*' questions to overcome this, e.g. *"What if there was enough time/budget?"* to get to the real objections.

- Help Topi evaluate the options, being careful that you do not do the judging for him. He needs to take ownership. Explore them objectively. You could use techniques like SWOT, weighing up pros and cons, or using a grid with columns that compares ease, timescale, resources etc.

Will

This is the Action Planning part of the process. Topi, with your help, needs to be able to address:

- What are you going to do?

- When are you going to do it?

- Will this action meet your goal?

- What obstacles might there be?

- Who needs to know?

- What support do you need and how will you get it?

- How will you know when you have been successful?

Using scales of 1-10 works well here too. You could ask Topi how certain he is that he will carry out the agreed action.

A clear, concise record of the agreed action should be produced. Some coaches prefer Topi to do this as it encourages ownership of the process.

This is the conclusion of the coaching process. You should help Topi realise what he has achieved. For example, he may have identified problems and found solutions, dropped unfounded opinions, or become more motivated to achieve success. You could ask Topi what he has got out of the coaching session, and then tell him some of your observations. Stick to the positive ones unless you want to start coaching all over again!

Ongoing support may include giving feedback, reviewing progress and valuing success.

Adapting to Topi

Beginning by identifying goals is not always the best starting point. In some situations it may be better to open by looking at the current situation (Reality), then moving on to ask Topi how he thinks things could be improved (Goals).

A good coach will have a flexible approach, responding to Topi's needs. He will recognise progress, be able to offer good advice, assess what else could be achieved, and identify or create learning opportunities.

Finally, coaches ask good questions, show genuine interest, listen well, encourage autonomy and understand the power and importance of developing others.

Warning!

- Don't just coach when things go wrong. You will get much more mileage for your efforts if you help Topi recognise and build on his strengths.

- Yes, it may be easier and quicker to do it yourself, but that won't get you staff that are motivated and committed, will it?

- Telling someone what to do, imposing your thoughts, being judgmental or emphasising weaknesses and failures is not coaching.

- Your aim is to encourage independence, not dependence on you.

7

Managing Conflict

Definition

An intervention aimed at finding a mutually agreed way forward when there are two opposing views, and emotions are impeding progress.

Outcomes

- Both people will have become aware of the thinking behind the position of the other, recognising their intent.

- The emotional responses of the other person will have been acknowledged.

- Common ground and mutual understanding will be identified, as well as areas where agreement cannot be found.

- A solution for coping with differences and compromising (where necessary) will be agreed.

Think Ahead

- Examine yourself first. Is your point of view based on fact, assumption or opinion? What emotions are you attaching to the situation?

- Do the same for Topi. Try to get a real understanding of the situation from his standpoint.

- What is at stake here? Work out potential outcomes, a worst case scenario and a best possible solution.

- Check facts and gather hard evidence where appropriate.

- How did it get to this? What were the triggers that caused the conflict?

- If there was a step by step way forward that mostly puts the onus on you to change, what would it be?

Steps

State the reason for the meeting, framing it positively and setting parameters of what you want to solve clearly.

Ask Topi to explain the situation from his point of view so you can check if your understanding of his positions and interests is accurate; you can also look for common ground.

Let Topi know you have heard. Acknowledge Topi's feelings. Name or describe them precisely as possible, so that you know what you are dealing with.

Give your point of view. Emphasise common ground, and mention your own feelings without over dramatising them or belittling Topi's.

Agree exactly what the problem is.

Ask Topi what he would like to be different. Work together to paint a picture of what the ideal scenario would be like.

Agree action points and behaviour changes that will help you both work towards an improved position.

Good Practice

Dealing with emotions

Conflict is sometimes predictable, never planned, and often erupts when you least expect it. So firstly, here are couple of tips on how to cope if an incident blows up and you are faced with a tirade of emotions.

You are likely to have an emotional response yourself; trying to settle the issue when feelings are running high on both sides is far from ideal, so avoid this if at all possible. Remember to acknowledge Topi's feelings "*I can see you're upset...*"

- Allow Topi to vent his feelings – as long as he isn't disturbing colleagues or customers, or threatening your safety.

- Check your body language, making a conscious effort to relax tense muscles so that you don't look defensive.

- Making a pacifying gesture, such as an apology, or expressing regret that Topi is upset, can help diffuse the situation. It doesn't mean you agree, just that you are sorry a colleague is distressed.

Your aim here is to buy your self a little time to allow emotions to abate, but you also need to ensure Topi knows that his concerns will be dealt with, so try to agree a time to sit down as talk as soon as you can. Just getting a cup of coffee may be enough if coming back to it later is not an option.

Practise out loud

Before the time comes, think carefully about what you want to say, and practise out loud – thinking about words isn't the same as actually speaking them. Your tone and pace are critical to success, which is why just thinking through the words you will use will not do the job.

Your aim is to express yourself calmly and firmly, bearing in mind that your response style will set the tone both for the discussion and for your future relationship.

Managing compromise

You will want to consider how far you are willing or able to compromise, where you can be flexible, and where – and why - you cannot.

What might the consequences be if the situation is not resolved? Is it a viable option? Sometimes, it is ok to agree that you have different views, and respect each other's right to hold their opinion.

Whatever the case, you will need to be able to explain your position clearly. If it is about facts, give the facts. Many misunderstandings occur because the full picture is not known. If it about your personality or preferences, say so. Trying to dress up your likes and dislikes as facts isn't honest and won't win you any respect.

Respect individuality

It is also important to recognise that people attach different values to situations, and so have a different emotional response. For example, you probably know people who get mad if their car parking space is taken, or their personal mug used, and others who are not in the slightest bit concerned. There is no right or wrong here.

You may need to agree on some levels of acceptable behaviour (there is a chapter on inappropriate behaviour), but you can't enforce your personal style or values on others and should not try to.

Conflict styles

You probably have a natural tendency to react in a certain way in a conflict situation.

Being aware of a range of possible responses, and selecting the most appropriate one for the situation is a good approach. Thomas and Kilmann identified five conflict styles, based on levels of assertiveness and cooperativeness. There is a short section on assertiveness in The Basics if you want to refresh your memory.

Competing

High assertiveness and low cooperativeness. You know what you want and you stand firm. This can come across as aggressive, confrontational and intimidating. It can be useful in a crisis or when you have to implement an unpopular decision. It is no use at all when trying to build or repair a relationship.

Collaborating

High assertiveness and high cooperativeness. The aim here is to find a win-win solution by taking into account both sets of needs. You are as willing to take on board Topi's needs as you are to express your own. It is a problem solving approach that can take time, but it is likely to lead to respect and trust.

Compromising

Moderate assertiveness and moderate cooperativeness. This style is about finding the middle ground, meeting Topi half way. You will be prepared to give some ground, and you will expect Topi to do the same – everyone is expected to be at least partly satisfied. This can be useful if a deadline is looming and a solution is needed quickly.

Accommodating

Low assertiveness and high cooperativeness. This means being willing to give up your own needs to meet those of others. Obviously this approach may not give you the best outcomes, but it is worth considering when the issue is more important to the other party than it is to you.

Avoiding

Low assertiveness and low cooperativeness - also known as seeking to avoid the issue! You may fall into this response if you do not want to hurt someone's feelings. It is usually an inappropriate response, but can be considered if winning is impossible or the conflict is trivial.

Can you spot your natural tendency, or think of examples of how you have coped with conflict in the past? What result might using a different style bring? Learning to review a situation objectively and choosing which response style to adopt will give you the best chance of success.

The top priority

You will have gathered by now that not letting emotions get the better of your thought processes is critical to success. Emotions muddle our judgement, often making us say things we don't mean, or saying what we do mean but in a manner we will regret later.

In most cases, Topi is not deliberately being difficult, but has different beliefs, values or understanding to you, which are as real and valid to him as yours are to you. Take another look at the Three-Step Tango technique in The Basics. It may well help.

The key thing is to make creating or maintaining a good relationship your top priority, by treating Topi courteously and with respect.

Warning!

- If you ignore conflict and hope it will go away, sometimes it does. But a lot of the time your avoidance feeds it further and it comes back stronger.

- Don't make promises for a quick solution you can't keep. It may be quick, but it will only damage your credibility when you don't deliver.

- Be aware of your competence and don't stray too far outside it. If you doubt your ability to handle a situation well, consider using a third person to mediate.

- You can learn from conflict, but don't hold grudges and dwell on it. Let it go – when it's over, it's over. Clinging to the upset only hurts you.

8

Managing The Dark Triad

Definition

A discussion that involves you standing your ground and protecting yourself with someone you suspect has a personality that borders on psychopathy, narcissism or **Machiavellianism** (known as The Dark Triad - definitions below).

Outcomes

- You are able to state your position and take action without being manipulated, blackmailed or made to feel guilty.

- You establish clear boundaries with Topi, protecting your own interests.

- You defend yourself against exploitation.

Think Ahead

- Do some homework about what is important to people with Topi's personality traits.

- Have a crystal clear understanding of your personal boundaries, and also what is acceptable in your workplace.

- Separate facts and actions from feelings and words. What is really going on?

- Rehearse your main points aloud, in a calm, firm voice.

- Think through how you will keep on track if Topi tries to divert the discussion.

- Be aware of how subtle manipulation can be, and what disguises it takes.

- Choose somewhere you feel safe to have the conversation. It is a good idea to have another person not too far away if you feel uncomfortable.

- They expect fight or flight. Give them neither. Practise ignoring their malicious energy.

- Weigh up pros against cons of working with them – they can be a mixed blessing.

Steps

- **Detach your emotions** so that you are less available to be manipulated. Hide your weak spots.

- **Use language that Topi can relate to**, i.e. always stating the positives and advantages from her point of view - as that is the only view she is interested in. What is in it for her?

- **Judge actions, not intentions**. Don't waste time trying to work out Topi's motives. What is she actually doing?

- **Speak up for yourself**, making your boundaries clear.

- **Make direct requests** and accept only direct responses. Avoid sarcasm and hostility.

- **Refuse to be drawn off topic**, do not respond to emotional blackmail. There is a technique called fogging that may work well for you – acknowledge their criticism without being drawn into discussing it, using phrases like *"that may be"*.

- **Don't make threats** – but do take actions swiftly when you need to.

- **Summarise** to reiterate your point.

- **Keep the conversation as short as possible**, being brief and businesslike, leaving them as little time as possible to try to get the upper hand.

Good Practice

Topi can't be swayed

This is not a book about personality disorders, but occasionally we need to deal with people who just don't exhibit what we consider normal, or good, behaviour.

In many chapters we extol the virtues of adapting our style, meeting Topi half way, or trying to understand her point of view and intent.

Sometimes, however, that just isn't going to work, because in this instance, Topi can't be swayed. She just was not built with a personality that allows her to empathise with others.

It's not you...

It's quite unlikely that you are a psychologist, or feel equipped to analyse Topi.

However, there are warning signs that you can identify that can give you the clue that the problem is not you – it's her.

If Topi is clever - and she usually is - she will be highly skilled at convincing you that you are a poor performer while she excels, or you are completely unreasonable and she, of course, is being very unfairly treated.

This chapter is here to help you wise up, accept that Topi can't be changed, and stop blaming yourself. There's no point blaming Topi, either, as she just can't help her psychological make up. Like all of us, though, she may have the ability to change her behaviour a little if she understands that it is to her advantage. Your job is to be consistently assertive and not allow yourself to be mistreated.

What is The Dark Triad?

The Dark Triad is a group of three personality traits:

• Narcissism

• Machiavellianism

• Psychopathy.

There are estimates that around 1% of the population have one or more of these traits. Any of them are likely to cause discord and difficulty in maintaining relationships.

There is often overlap between the three, so you may find elements of one, two or even all three in one individual.

Let's look at some of the character traits involved:

The Narcissist

• Has an inflated ego, with an unrealistic sense of her own self importance

• Has fantasies of power, and needs power to survive

• Needs admiration

• Has an entrenched sense of entitlement

• Is hyper sensitive to criticism

• Deeply believes she should be the centre of attention

• Can turn hostile and aggressive if she feels her ego is threatened.

The Psychopath

• Uses superficial charm

• Has no remorse or guilt

• Has no conscience

- Behaves impulsively

- Is a pathological liar

- Exploits colleagues without shame or guilt

- Is emotionally ice cold

- Acts ruthlessly.

The Machiavellian

- Deceives and manipulates for their own gain

- Disregards morality

- Enjoys conning you and scheming

- Will act unscrupulously

- Gets pleasure from causing your downfall.

Empathy? What empathy?

The common thread between all three is innate self-centredness. They all have very high levels of self-interest, are usually bold and confident, and have low or non existent levels of empathy. If they're working for the good of the business it's only because it happens to be in line with their personal aims.

They are only interested in you if you can help them meet their own goals. They genuinely do not have the capacity to take your point of view on board; reciprocity is alien to them.

Consequently, they are not good at sustaining long term relationships. They can thrive in a work environment that is constantly changing or moving around, as they are never in one place or position long enough to be challenged or sacked. They will get by anywhere they can find admirers to feed their egos.

They make ruthless bosses. You are unlikely to maintain a long-term working relationship with one of them unless you are very tolerant or prepared to be subservient to them.

How they work

Even if you have never encountered one of these characters you can probably predict the impact they can have. They have a whole arsenal of psychological weapons to get to your emotions so that they can manipulate and control.

They can sap your energy, destroy trust, derail careers, and raise unwanted emotions. They may seem endlessly charming, be capable orators, appear to be on your side, and be very supportive as long as you are giving them whatever it is they want.

Their aggression is not always obvious; it can take quite a while before you realise what is going on. Have you been fooled? Do you feel uneasy, or under pressure? Is the 'concern' your colleague has been showing just a covert form of bullying?

Often they use the tactic of appearing 'hurt' themselves, in a bid to get your sympathy. Our object here, sadly, is to protect you and limit the damage Topi can cause, rather than reach an amicable understanding.

This is just a peek into a huge topic, and one you can read about endlessly.

You can't fix it...

The bottom line is that if Topi does have these personality traits, you can't fix her. Aim to limit the damage she causes rather than expect her to respond as well as others do to your support and encouragement.

...but you can manage it

You may be able to establish and uphold boundaries, particularly if you are not standing in between Topi and what she wants, but that is as good as it gets.

It may be that even though Topi is difficult to work with, she may be superb at her job, particularly if it involves charming clients or holding her nerve. In this case it is in your best interests to find a way you can work together.

Of course, as with any colleague, you will aim to treat her with respect and fairness. In addition:

• Be wary of responding to friendly overtures. You will be better protected by keeping your relationship on a purely professional basis.

• You may be able to get her compliance by giving her flattery, and all the admiration she feels she deserves. Make her seem central to any project or meeting you suggest. It is your judgement call whether this approach will work for you.

• Be more alert than usual to being led down a path. What appears to be friendly banter or a genuine sob story are attempts to win over your emotions – giving Topi the control she wants.

The only sure fire way of removing Topi's impact is to get out of the situation, or get her out of it.

This may seem extreme, especially if it involves leaving your job. Only you can assess the circumstances. If the situation is serious, get advice.

• If Topi is out of order in the workplace, involve HR professionals.

• If Topi is a subordinate, weigh up her usefulness to the organisation against the trouble she causes.

• If she is your boss, will the culture of the organisation allow her to thrive, or will she be ousted? You can hang on, or you can save your sanity by looking for a new role elsewhere.

Honestly and thoughtfully, weigh up the impact Topi is having on your life, and decide what you can tolerate without it affecting your wellbeing. Your health is the bottom line, and you should protect it at all costs.

Warning!

- All personality traits are a spectrum, and we're all on them somewhere. Just because someone portrays the odd tantrum or outburst, it doesn't necessarily make them a founder member of The Dark Triad. Don't jump to conclusions, but do observe actions.

- Where are you on the spectrum? Do you find it difficult to appreciate a different point of view? Do you think you are surrounded by incompetence? Is it possible that others see you as belonging to The Dark Triad?

- Beware of labels. You may have gathered enough evidence and researched enough to convince you what you are dealing with, but unless you happen to be a clinical psychologist you are not qualified to say for sure.

- Are you a natural rescuer, convinced that everyone can be won round eventually by love and understanding? You could be wasting a huge amount of energy that could be used supporting someone who will actually appreciate it.

9

Delegating

Definition

Giving responsibility for completing a task or project to a colleague, usually from the top down.

Outcomes

- The task is completed in line with the instructions given.

- You give Topi an opportunity to perform and develop his skills.

- Topi acquires broader skills and knowledge and becomes more useful.

- The breadth of tasks you can delegate in the future grows.

Think Ahead

- Have you chosen the right person? What other options do you have?

- Has Topi currently got the necessary skills, or the aptitude to develop them?

- How much freedom should you give to Topi? What control is it wise to retain?

- How much initiative do you want Topi to use?

- Who else needs to know?

- How will you explain the task so that Topi understands? How could your instructions be misunderstood?

Steps

- **Explain** why the task needs doing and why you have chosen Topi to do it.

- **Find out** how Topi feels about the task. Is he happy to rise to the challenge? Does he have any fears or concerns?

- **Give details** about what exactly needs doing by when, including any flexibility there is.

- **Ask if Topi has any questions**. His questions will help you discover his understanding of what you have said. If he has no questions, ask him to explain back to you what needs doing, so that you can check that you have communicated clearly, with no room for misunderstanding.

- **Make sure Topi understands** the outcome you are looking to achieve, and how the task fits into the wider picture.

- **Define your decision making processes.** What can Topi decide, and what should he defer to you?

- **Say when you need progress reports** and how you will monitor him.

Good Practice

Delegation can make or break working relationships. If it is done well Topi feels trusted, involved and motivated, and develops more respect for you. On the other hand, if it is done badly Topi may feel put upon, used and confused – in which case his opinion of you, and his performance, plummets.

A balancing act

In addition to giving clear and complete instructions, the key to successful delegation lies in achieving a balancing act.

You have a set of requirements, e.g. a need for information on progress, how you want the task done, and how much freedom you are prepared to give.

Meanwhile, Topi requires a level of support, the authority to proceed, and the confidence to get the job done.

A clear understanding of both sides will lead to successful delegation. Think of an example:

- What are your requirements?

- What are Topi's requirements?

If the needs of both sides cannot be met, the delegated task could well run into trouble.

Delegation is one of those areas where you do need to flex your approach, depending on the circumstance. The chapter on Instructing may be useful too.

The task

You will need to consider:

- The **size** of the task. Has Topi the capacity, or will some of his other duties need to be offloaded somehow?

- The **importance** of the task. The more important the task, the more effort you will put into making sure it is done well.

- The **urgency** of the task. Can Topi get it done quicker than anyone else? He may be able to do it to the highest standard, but every now and then speed is more important than quality.

- The **uniqueness** of the task. The more unusual it is, the more you will need to think about how it needs to be done. Do you need to be prescriptive? Does it require a creative approach? Does it matter how it is done? Does the organisation have the necessary skills and experience among its people?

- The **resources** the task requires. If you cannot equip Topi with the resources he needs, you are setting him up for failure.

About Topi...

You will need to ask yourself:

- How much **experience** of the task does Topi have? You need to gauge this well to decide how much support and input he will require.

- What is Topi's level of **confidence** in the skills involved? In an ideal world, we would all feel assured about things we were able to do well. Unfortunately this is not always the case, and may have a bearing on how much time and support we need to give. This is not a reason to pass Topi over in favour of a more confident person; rather it is an opportunity to get Topi's confidence levels raised which ultimately will make your job easier.

- What **skills and attributes** will Topi need? Will the task help him develop and grow, so that he is more useful to you in the future?

While Topi is working

- Make sure that **monitoring** and follow up takes Topi's needs into account, and not just yours. You might feel the need to check how it's going hourly; Topi will think you do not trust him and see you as meddlesome.

- Ensure **timely problem solving.** Make sure Topi knows what to do if he hits a snag.

- Take time for **reviewing** how it went afterwards. Again, the scale of the review depends on the size and nature of the task. It could take a minute, or a couple of hours. This is your opportunity to help Topi realise his strengths and capabilities, which should in turn motivate him to continue improving and taking on challenges. You'll also have a more useful member of staff.

If you pay attention to all the above your chances of success are good.

There are times, of course, when unexpected circumstances stop plans working out. When you are reviewing with Topi, bear in mind that we learn far more from our failures than our successes, and be sure not to blame Topi for things outside his control.

Warning!

- If you just delegate the dull or difficult tasks you don't want to do, what impact do you think that has on Topi's motivation? Or opinion of you?

- Have you ever met anyone who finds being micromanaged in any way desirable?

- If you provide a vague, broad brief, it's likely you'll get a vague, muddled result.

- Topi will only respond to your brief if he thinks you have the authority to pass the work on. Is this clear, or are you assuming?

- If you are a perfectionist, or set in your ways, it is unlikely that any living person will carry out the task exactly the same as you would, to your exacting standards. Be careful that Topi isn't made to feel a failure because you are setting the bar impossibly high.

10

Disciplinary Meetings

Definition

A formal meeting to make Topi aware that his work performance or behaviour has fallen below an acceptable level, and that there will be consequences if he does not rectify the situation. Informal attempts to rectify the situation will have already occurred.

Outcomes

- You have explained precisely to Topi the performance or behaviour that is below standard, and what the outcomes will be for Topi if it continues.

- You have in place the procedures to follow through if necessary.

- Topi knows exactly what the repercussion will be if he repeats the behaviour or does not improve his work.

- A record of the discussion has been produced in writing.

Think Ahead

- Is it possible that Topi is unclear about what standards are required from him?

- Is it possible that there are other factors preventing Topi from performing well?

- Where is the required standard documented? Is Topi's job description thorough enough? Is there a competency framework that describes what behaviours are wanted – and which are not?

- What hard evidence do you have that Topi has underperformed? Have you seen or heard it yourself? Has it been documented? Could you get more evidence from a different source to make your case more convincing?

- Has Topi already been made aware of the issue informally, such as through regular supervision? It is not usual – unless the offence is very serious – to have a disciplinary meeting without the problem being mentioned previously, to give Topi time to solve it before formal proceedings begin.

- What would your preferred outcome be? What options are open to you? Could Topi be a reasonable worker in another part of the company?

- Are you up to date with employment law regarding disciplinary procedures?

- Timing is important. You will need some time to gather evidence – Topi will want to prepare his evidence or defence too – but the issue should be dealt with fairly swiftly while it is still recent.

Steps

- **Inform Topi in writing** of the disciplinary meeting. You should offer him the opportunity to bring another person, such as a colleague or Union Representative with him if he wishes.

- **Hold the meeting** with Topi to discuss the problem in a quiet, private environment that is free from distractions.

- **Keeping your tone calm** and businesslike, explain the problem to Topi and go through the evidence with him.

- **Give Topi an opportunity to ask questions**, respond to the allegations, and present his case. He should also be able to call for witnesses if appropriate.

- **Explain clearly what improvement is needed**, and what will happen if it does not occur.

- **Tell Topi that he is able to appeal** against your decision when you make it if he wishes; you don't have to reach a decision then and there.

- **Adjourn the meeting** to give yourself time to consider the evidence and mitigating circumstances. Let Topi know when he can expect to hear what your next step will be.

- **Close the meeting** and ensure that you record key facts.

Good Practice

You'll be aware how important it is that a disciplinary meeting should not be the first time that Topi hears there is a problem, unless he has done something serious and rapid action needs to be taken.

Many potential disciplinary issues can be resolved informally; if you need to back track a little, see the chapters on performance gaps or inappropriate behaviour.

Sometimes it is appropriate to have a fact finding meeting first, to establish what is going on before you move to formal disciplinary procedures.

Is this the only way?

Do your best to think around the problem to find a solution. It may be that Topi is a square peg in a round hole, has some behavioural issues, or is just not able to acquire the skills he needs. Here are some questions that might help:

- Are there parts of the role that Topi performs well? Are these skills valuable to the company?

- Is any part of the problem caused by the environment or people in it? What variables could be changed?

- If it is a skills issue, how many methods have been tried to help him learn? Is there an underlying issue, such as dyslexia or poor retention?

Know the law

As there are different reasons for disciplining someone, some more serious than others, formal disciplinary meetings can be a bit of a minefield unless you are very sure about employment legislation.

If you have a Human Resource adviser or department in your organisation, do keep them informed so that they can support you and make sure you are following procedures correctly. If you are a small company, find an external HR professional to help and guide you.

Even if you consider the meeting to be a verbal warning (which is sometimes know as the first stage), it still needs to be recorded in writing. You should record:

- The complaint against Topi

- Topi's defence

- Findings made and actions taken

You can then add to your record as the case progresses. If Topi does not or cannot improve to the standard you require after a reasonable amount of time, you will need to issue a formal written warning at a second meeting (stage two). HR professionals can advise of your options at this point, including how to dismiss Topi if no other way forward can be found.

Also do bear in mind that if you are involved in the case, you cannot be the person who investigates it or carries out the meeting. It is quite usual to get an external HR professional to manage the process.

Fair treatment

It is important to treat Topi fairly, so consider the following points:

- Be prompt in your handling of the matter, and do not delay or postpone meetings.

- Try not to let your own worries or emotions about handling this cloud your judgement or affect the meeting. Remain objective, fair and level headed.

- Make sure you behave consistently across staff. Is Topi being singled out in some way?

- Investigate properly – do not rely on hearsay, especially where personality clashes are involved.

- Topi may need time to think before he responds, so give him some time to answer the case.

If it is you who is being disciplined...

You should be given an opportunity to explain your side of the situation, so ask for this if it is not offered.

Try to keep your emotions under control so that you can give a reasoned explanation of why things went wrong. This will also help you keep it in perspective. Is it one aspect of your performance that is under the microscope, or are you just in the wrong job?

Think through what you would like to happen – do you want to keep this job? If so, what changes need to be made so that you can thrive? Your manager will appreciate it if you attend the meeting with some constructive ideas, and the willingness to accept your faults.

If you are struggling with the situation, contact ACAS (The Advisory and Conciliation Service). They have a good range of resources available online, and also have a helpline that can give you advice and support.

The chapter on giving feedback may also help.

Warning!

- Topi could take you to a tribunal if you do not follow the correct procedures.

- Think about the wider reputation of your organisation. Some companies seem to have a gung ho 'hire 'em and fire 'em' approach to disciplining all and sundry, while others avoid it and let all kinds of bad behaviour carry on. Are you happy that you have found a model of best practice in your approach?

Dismissing a Member of Staff

Definition

A formal meeting where a member of staff is told that their contract of employment is being terminated, for one of the reasons allowed by law, outlined below.

Outcomes

- Topi knows that her employment has been terminated and has been given confirmation in writing.

- You have informed Topi, clearly and professionally, that she no longer has a job with the company, and the notice she is required to serve.

Think Ahead

- Have you checked that you have legal grounds to dismiss Topi? Have all necessary procedures been followed?

- Have you worked out how much wages and holiday pay Topi is owed? Has payment been arranged?

- Do you expect Topi to work out her notice or leave immediately? Prepare a letter that tells Topi this and any other information she needs.

- Given the circumstances, what manner should you adopt?

- How do you expect Topi to react to the news?

- What is the best time and place to break the news?

- What exactly are you going to say? Write yourself notes or a script if it helps, and rehearse if you are nervous. It needs to be clear and simple.

- If you think Topi might react badly, have another person on standby to offer some support afterwards

Steps

- **Explain that Topi's employment is being terminated** and the reason why. Keep it reasonably brief, factual and business like.

- **Ask Topi if she has anything she wants to say or ask.** Address any questions but try not to get drawn into a lengthy debate or slanging match.

- **Give Topi some time** to come to terms with the news.

- **Explain any arrangements** such as outstanding pay, notice period, and give Topi confirmation in writing.

- **Tell her what happens next.** Can she go home or clear her desk? Thank her for her time.

Good Practice

Check the law

As with several subjects in this book, it is crucial that you ensure that you are within the law, and have followed the correct procedures. The only legal reasons for dismissing Topi are:

- Misconduct

- Gross misconduct

- Inability to perform

- Redundancy (see the chapter on making someone redundant)

- A statutory requirement, such as a driver losing their licence.

- Some other substantial reason, e.g. the role was a temporary position.

Using any other reason could result in you being taken to a tribunal for unfair dismissal. In fact, you could end up in a tribunal even if you have a valid case if you have not used the correct processes. If you are not absolutely sure of your ground, a HR professional or ACAS will be able to advise you.

You will need to think about your approach. For example, if there has been gross misconduct you will want to act very swiftly and dismiss Topi quickly, as she could potentially cause further damage.

It is possible that you would prefer for Topi to work her notice to give you time to find a replacement if, for example, Topi is just not quite up to the standard required, and you have tried coaching and training have been through the process verbal and written warnings.

How to behave

The law may be relatively easy to define, but how you handle the conversation to some extent depends on the circumstances. You should always have a professional manner: avoid waffling and beating round the bush, or being so abrupt that it is over before Topi knows what has hit her.

You may want to be reasonably friendly in tone if Topi is expecting the news, and has been cooperative in the process of trying reach the right standard. On the other hand, if she has been disruptive or behaved very badly you may prefer to take a more detached stance.

How will Topi respond?

Be prepared for anger or upset. Your message may brief but that does not necessarily mean you can expect a very short meeting. It is a temptation to get it over and done with as quickly as possible to save yourself from dealing with the fallout, but in reality you will may need to allow some time for Topi to vent, come to terms with it and compose herself. Remain calm, give her space and don't feel you need to fill every silence.

The bottom line is that Topi is not the right person for the job, so you would be doing her no favours by keeping her on. She may not see right now that you are freeing her to find a role that will suit her better, and so be better for her wellbeing, but often that is really the case.

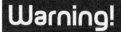

Warning!

- Don't go on about how bad you feel about dismissing Topi. This is not about you. She is unlikely to have much sympathy.

- If you haven't given Topi appropriate warnings and guidance she could take you to an industrial tribunal. I am sure you have better things to do with your time.

- If Topi is volatile, do remember that emotions can cloud judgement. You will have heard tales of the bizarre things that people sometimes do when they are dismissed, which sometimes includes sabotage by destroying files or sending inappropriate emails. It can seem harsh to ask Topi to leave the premises immediately, but you do need to weigh up the risk.

Exit Interviews

Definition

An interview carried out with an employee who is leaving the organisation, to inform the employer about factors that influenced the decision to leave and the employee's experience of working for the company.

Outcomes

* The employer has explored and verified Topi's reasons for leaving.

* The employer is able to organise knowledge transfer, if Topi needs to pass on information.

* Topi has had an opportunity to give comment on what it was like working for the organisation.

* Both sides are able to contribute to making sure that Topi leaves on good terms.

Think Ahead

- If your organisation does not have an exit questionnaire, prepare a list of questions you want to ask. What information would be useful to you? Many examples are available online.

- To make it easier to analyse the results when you have a number of responses it is a good idea to make sure you can measure them where possible, i.e. *"On a scale of 1-10 how would you rate..."* rather than *"How do you feel about...'"*

- Book a time and venue as soon as possible.

- Allow sufficient time. It will be hard to get the information you want once Topi has gone.

Steps

- Outline the reason for the meeting, how long it will take and what will happen to the information that Topi gives you.

- Explain the subject areas you want to discuss with Topi, and any paperwork you are using.

- Work logically through the questions you have prepared. Make sure that you explore Topi's answers (e.g. *"What makes you say that?"* or *"Can you tell me a little more about that?")* so that you get the full picture and understand things from Topi's point of view.

- Remain impartial and objective so that you don't get drawn into disagreements or being defensive.

- Ask Topi if there is anything else he would like to tell you that could help the organisation to be a better place to work.

- Thank Topi for his time and wish him well for the future

Good Practice

Most large organisations use exit interviews as a way of collecting data that can be used to help them improve working conditions, or even inform bigger, more strategic decisions.

Studies show that they do help improve staff retention and reveal useful information.

Even if you work for a very small company it could still be worth your while carrying out exit interviews and recording your findings. Replacing Topi is an expensive business, so the less often you have to do it the better it is for a company.

Your aim is two fold:

- **Interpersonal** You have a meaningful conversation that leaves Topi feeling that he has had the opportunity to say all he we wants to about leaving the company, and you feel you really understand what it has been like in Topi's shoes.

- **Informative** You understand better how to help the strategic direction of the company, by identifying changes that could be made to lead to a more engaged workforce.

It's always worth grasping the nettle

Some people shy away from exit interviews as they think that Topi will take the opportunity to complain and moan about the way he has been treated. In reality, this is rarely the case.

Even if it does go this way, it is important for the employer to understand what has occurred so that steps can be put into place to stop it happening again.

It is also a great chance to make sure that your working relationship ends constructively. You may think that it does not matter, because you will never see Topi again, but of course there is the possibility that at some time in the future your paths will cross.

It is also understandable that you will balk at the thought of an exit interview if you have been responsible for Topi leaving. If you have dismissed him or made him redundant, for example, you'll already know why he is leaving!

In this case you may need to adjust your approach, but there is still merit in going ahead for two reasons:

• Fairness if other staff are getting exit interviews

• Topi may still have valid comments on how the company does things, which may reinforce or add to information you already have.

Getting the most out of the interview

Do pay particular attention to your tone, body language and manner.

It is important that you create an environment where Topi is able to say difficult things. Be calm and fair, as you may need to be gentle and coax the truth out – after all, if everything was perfect, would he be leaving? If you appear rushed, brusque or disinterested, Topi is likely to conclude that you are doing a form filling exercise and have no real concern for his views.

Be sure that your exit interviews are not just a bureaucratic exercise; this is always the temptation when a questionnaire is in front of you, particularly when the questionnaire is asking for numbers or yes and no answers. Think about the actual words you use to ask the question. Take the opportunity really to understand the reasons behind Topi leaving you, and consider whether the company realistically could have done more to encourage Topi to stay.

Most of all make sure that you are listening more than talking. It is good practice to ask open questions and discuss the subject in hand before asking Topi for a score of out of 10 where you need one. If you do this, you are much more likely to get a true answer and better understanding of Topi's point of view.

If you don't already have an exit questionnaire, look at examples and select the questions that will work well in your organisation. Even if you do already have one, it is worth regularly considering if it is fit for purpose. You can do this by making a list of the information you want to collect, and then checking to see if your form covers the ground.

You will want some questions around how you can put things right or prevent them from going wrong in the future, and others around what improvement opportunities Topi can suggest.

Here are a few example questions you can adapt or build on to suit:

The resignation

- Can you explain why you've decided to leave? (If appropriate: Why is this important to you?)

- What is your main reason for leaving?

- Are there any other reasons for your leaving?

- What could have been done to make it possible for you to stay with us?

- What could we have handled differently?

Time with the company

- How do you feel about the company?

- What has been good about working here?

- What could we have done better?

- What would you have liked to be able to do during your time here that you were not able to (e.g. extra responsibilities)?

- How could we have helped you reach your potential?

- How well did we assess and meet your training needs?

- How effective was your appraisal? How relevant were objectives set?

- Do you have any suggestions for improvements we can make?

- Can you comment on how you have been managed?

- How would you describe the culture of the company?

Issues at work

- Were there any issues in the workplace that contributed to your decision to leave?

- How could these issues have been resolved?

- Do you have any comments on our procedures that would help us solve problems in the future?

- Do you have any health and safety concerns about our premises?

- What could we do to reduce stress levels at work?

- Is there anything we do that you view as valueless (e.g. unnecessary reports, rules or bureaucracy)?

- Do you have any comments about your treatment here from a discrimination, bullying or harassment perspective?

The future

- Would you consider working for us again in the future?

- Are you happy to tell us where you are going?

- What is it that makes you want to join them?

- What are they offering that we are not?

As you can see, these are broad questions that need tailoring and expanding to meet your needs, and also need a scoring mechanism added where appropriate.

If it is your exit interview...

Do put some thought into deciding what it would be useful for the company to hear.

What is hard fact, and what is just your opinion? If the culture doesn't suit your personality, it isn't necessarily anyone's fault.

Try and leave on good terms. Do not use it as an opportunity to let off steam – it could backfire further down the line.

Warning!

- You may be part of the problem! Although it is usual for the line manager to carry out exit interviews because they know the role best, sometimes it is better to let an impartial person from another part of the business to do it. HR professionals may be able to help.

- There is little point carrying out an exit interview if you are not going to consider the information you gain seriously. Remember, though, that it is one employee's perspective. You will need stronger evidence before you can view it as fact.

13
Feedback

Definition

Giving feedback is letting people know how they are doing at work. It may be about just a small part of their role, or about how they do something rather than what they do. It can positive, negative, or neutral (for example, *"You take a very unusual approach to..."*). There is a separate chapter that covers dealing with performance gaps; here we are just considering the aspect of feedback.

Receiving feedback is being told how you are performing at work – we'll come to this at the end of the chapter, and concentrate on giving feedback first.

Outcomes

- You have had the opportunity to give feedback to Topi in a manner that helps her accept and understand your perception of an issue.

- Topi has a clear understanding of how aspects of her work are viewed by you.

- Topi has increased her self-awareness.

Think Ahead

- What will be achieved by giving the feedback? If there is nothing to be gained, is there any reason for giving feedback at all?

- What does wanting to give the feedback tell you about your own attitude, values and beliefs? Always consider your own motives.

- What possible emotional reactions may Topi have? And how will you respond? You might not guess right, but thinking through the possibilities is part of preparation.

- Clarify exactly what it is you want to say. Make sure you eliminate assumptions and stick to reality.

- Think about where you will give the feedback, bearing in mind how Topi may respond.

- Consider timing. Feedback should be fresh and timely – but not immediate if there is anger or upset that needs to be allowed to settle.

Steps

- **State or reiterate the reason for the meeting** and describe the issue you are giving feedback on.

- **If appropriate, ask Topi for her views** on what happened. If she has a perception that matches yours, you won't need to give feedback. If it doesn't, at least you know what you are dealing with.

- **Listen carefully** to what Topi says, and observe her body language. There is a chance that you might review your feedback if she presents new evidence.

- **Give the feedback clearly and calmly**. Do not rush, uses pauses to allow Topi to absorb what you are saying.

- **Ask Topi if she agrees with the feedback.** If she does not, you may need to explain more fully, or in a different way.

- **Let Topi know what the impact on the business** and workmates or colleagues has been.

- **Check that Topi understands the feedback** and has kept a healthy sense of perspective before you close the discussion.

Good Practice

Feedback is an essential part of learning. It is important to consider the impact of the message you are sending and the affect it will have on Topi. Sometimes it is necessary to deliver negative information, but even in this case the underlying approach should be supportive and objective.

The key issue when giving or receiving feedback is to keep the dialogue focused on the behaviour, not to reject the person displaying the behaviour, or feel rejected yourself. Remember to *"attack the problem, not the person"*. You may also need to help Topi keep the feedback in perspective.

When giving feedback, you will need to:

- **Listen.** If you have not listened and fully understood the situation, you are not in a position to comment.

- **Acknowledge** the other person and give positive reinforcement, perhaps by mentioning their strong points or value as a colleague.

- **Be supportive** in manner - do not attempt to give feedback when feelings are running high.

- **Use an appropriate amount of emphasis.** Find the middle ground between being too soft and coming down like a ton of bricks, and adapt according to the gravity of the issue. How much detail is required for optimum effectiveness?

- **Be Specific.** Be truthful and straightforward, and sure of the facts of what you are going to say. Give specific examples of the behaviour that you are commenting on. Say honestly what the effects and consequences of this behaviour are.

- **Work toward an outcome.** You may not have all the answers, but if you are giving criticism it should be constructive. State what changes you would realistically like to see, and suggest how they could be implemented. Offer an analysis of the issue as you see it, but be prepared to alter your perception. See the chapter on Performance Gaps for guidance.

- **Consider feelings.** How might the news you are delivering be received emotionally? What range of emotional responses do you expect from Topi? Are you in the right frame of mind to be able to give constructive feedback? Use your awareness of her body language to adjust your approach.

- **Order your message** so that it is logical from Topi's viewpoint. Try to start and finish on a positive note. Keep to the subject in hand – do not introduce other issues or get distracted as this will weaken your effectiveness.

- **Select the right environment.** Choose your timing and venue carefully. Is it conducive to the type of conversation you want? Is it free from interruptions? Who could overhear? Nobody wants to be criticised in public.

- **Tone.** Choose an appropriate tone of voice to deliver your message, and back it up with body language that conveys the same meaning. Keep your approach in proportion to the message you are delivering.

- **Clarify understanding.** Never assume that the message given is the message received. Make sure that the other person understands what you are saying, and is not adding anything you did not intend.

Receiving feedback

Sometimes, the boot is on the other foot and we are on the receiving end of feedback. This requires us to have an open mind and a desire for self-improvement. Your natural reaction might be to be defensive, apologise, or feel totally rejected. You may need to use your listening and questioning skills to identify the behaviour that is being discussed. Remember that your behaviour or actions may cause criticism, but you are still a human being of equal value!

- Get the full picture, including specific examples of the behaviour being discussed. Ask for evidence, illustrations, and incidents.

- Accept the information for what it is – the other person's perception of your performance.

- Check your understanding of the issue by feeding it back to the other person. *"So what you are saying is..."*

- Think carefully before you respond - it may not be best to go with your first instinct.

- You have the choice of accepting the feedback, rejecting it, or accepting part of it.

- If you accept the feedback, you may decide you should change your behaviour. However, it does not mean that you have to. If the behaviour is not affecting anyone else, and does not have an impact on your obligations, e.g. your work performance, you can note the feedback and choose not to act on it.

- If the feedback is not justified, do not accept it. You can put forward your case to explain why it is not fair or true, or you can tell the other person if they are overstepping limits such as giving personal or exaggerated criticism.

- You can choose not to engage in a dialogue if you wish, and a technique called fogging can help you achieve this. Fogging is acknowledging the criticism or statement without agreeing or disagreeing, and moving swiftly to another subject. You might use phrases like *"That may be"*, *"Thank you for bringing it to my attention"*, or *"I can see how you might think that"*.

- Delaying can be useful. If you feel unprepared to enter a discussion, prefer to engage with a more positive frame of mind, or if you need time to consider what you have been told, postpone your response until a better time.

Warning!

- Why should Topi listen to you? Are you the right person to give her feedback? It could be very hard going if you do not already have a good working relationship.

- Giving feedback should always be handled sensitively. We may do our best to predict someone's reaction, but we are not always aware of Topi's Achilles heel. Proceed with caution; you can always increase the firmness of your tone, but it is difficult to back down if you have gone in too strongly.

14

Grievances

Definition

A meeting where one member of staff raises a concern, complaint or problem about how they have been treated with a more senior member of staff. The grievance only becomes a formal procedure if the matter has previously been raised informally but not been resolved, and the person with the grievance puts it in writing. When it reaches this stage, the meeting is called a hearing.

Outcomes

- The area of concern is out in the open, and can be acted upon as appropriate.

- The junior person has expressed concerns, and given evidence to support his claims.

- The senior person has understood the complaint, and outlined how it will be dealt with.

- A way forward is identified (which at first may simply be further investigation) and confirmed in writing.

Think Ahead

If you are receiving the grievance...

- While you should be curious to find out exactly what has happened, you need to reserve judgement until after you have heard what Topi has to say, and have investigated his allegations fully.

- Are you the right person to be hearing the grievance? If you are part of the problem you cannot be involved in the hearing – it needs to be an impartial person. If your company is very small you may need to use an external HR professional.

- Read through your company's grievance procedure to make sure that you apply it correctly.

- Make sure you are up to date with employees' rights and grievance procedures. ACAS or an HR professional will be able to help.

- Gather any relevant facts or paperwork.

- It is important to get to the truth, so make sure you make it easy for Topi to speak openly. Choose a private space where you will not be interrupted or distracted.

- What questions will you ask to get to the heart of the matter?

- Do you want a witness present, who can verify that the meeting was handled properly? A witness can also help by taking notes.

- Give Topi plenty of notice of the meeting so he can prepare his case, and remind him that he can be accompanied if he wishes. Do read up on appropriate people to attend with Topi; for example it should not be someone who can prejudice the hearing.

If you are making the grievance...

- Have you gathered all the evidence you possibly can to support your case?

- How can you quantify the impact of your grievance? For example, how long has it been going on, how many people are affected, how does it impact on productivity etc.

- Does the way you have been treated contravene any law or company policy? Finding out is part of your preparation.

- View your facts from all angles. How could they be interpreted or misunderstood by others?

- You need to express what you have to say in a way that Topi will understand it. Think carefully about how you will tell your story. Often a straightforward chronological approach is the easiest way. Another technique is to start with the headline, i.e. the impact of what has happened, and then explain what led up to the grievance.

- How will you make sure that your emotions don't hijack the meeting?

- You could take another person with you, such as a colleague or union representative. Would you like to do this? If so, you need to make a reasonable request to do so i.e. choose someone who will not prejudice the meeting. Check this out with ACAS guidelines to see how this works.

- What outcome or outcomes are you looking for? What compromises would you be prepared to make?

Steps

If you are hearing a grievance:

- **Assure Topi** that you will give him the opportunity to present his grievance, and that any information he gives you will be kept confidentially.

- **Ask Topi to explain** the grievance. Let him say all that he wants to. Acknowledge his feelings.

- **Ask questions** to help you understand exactly what has happened, who or what is involved, and what the impact has been.

- **Summarise the situation.** Ask Topi if your understanding is correct, and if there is anything else he wishes to say. Let Topi correct or add to your understanding.

- **Ask Topi how he would like to see the situation resolved**. Listen to his ideas, comment on what is and what may not be possible if appropriate.

- **Say what you intend to do next.** Depending on the nature of the grievance, the right action may be obvious. Usually, however, you will need to think it through, talk to people or investigate further, in which case tell Topi when you will get back to him.

- **If appropriate, offer Topi extra support** until the situation is resolved.

- **Make notes** that summarise the meeting, and make sure that Topi gets a copy.

Good Practice

A grievance can be any complaint, concern or problem that an employee wishes to raise with management with the intention of resolving it. Often disputes can be settled informally, but if an employee is not satisfied, they should begin a formal process by putting their grievance in writing.

There is plenty of guidance available online about both sides' responsibilities, so do make sure that you follow the correct procedure. Seek advice from ACAS, an HR professional or a Union Representative if you need to.

If you are hearing a grievance:

Firstly, remember that for many people it takes a lot of courage to raise a grievance. Most of us don't like to admit we have a problem, and especially that we don't know how to solve it. From your point of view, you may think that Topi is overreacting or getting things out of proportion.

Whatever the outcome of the grievance dispute, do take into account that Topi's feelings are real to him. You can acknowledge how he feels (*"I can see that you are very upset..."*) without voicing an opinion on the matter in hand. If you dismiss the issue as trivial, you are likely to make Topi's negative feelings grow, not shrink. It is real to him.

If you want to help Topi see the wider picture, or get things in perspective, the best place to start is understanding it through his eyes. Listen, and explore, as the Three Step Tango model in The Basics suggests, until you can fully understand it from his standpoint. From there, you can think about how you can help him to see other information, or gently challenge his perceptions.

The most important thing, of course, is that Topi's bravery in raising the issue is rewarded, and that not only does he feel heard but also he has confidence that the right outcome will prevail.

Confirm the nature of the grievance and the agreed action in writing as soon as possible. If it is a formal grievance you also need to let Topi know that he has the right to appeal.

If you have a grievance:

It is highly likely that if you have a grievance it will have upset you in some way because you think you have not been treated well. You may feel angry, stressed, anxious, belittled, or any one of a host of other emotions. Letting the emotional impact on you be seen may be part of presenting the grievance, but do not let your upset or temper detract from making sure the facts are understood.

Our emotions have a funny way of interfering with our rational thought processes and our ability to express ourselves coherently, so it is worth thinking about how you can stop this happening.

Here are a couple of ideas:

- Practise what you want to say, preferably in front of a trusted friend who can give you some feedback on whether you were clear and easy to understand.

- Make notes of your main points in a logical order, and refer to them if you lose your thread or go blank.

It is natural to have emotions, so do not worry too much if they do show; just make sure that the facts of the case are evident too. Also, if you have read The Basics, you will know that it may help your cause to take into consideration how Topi prefers to communicate. Can you adapt your language or approach to more closely match his?

Warning

- Don't be defensive. It can be hard to hear your company, department or a trusted colleague criticised, but keep your emotional response in check and remain objective.

- It might be easy to sweep this one under the carpet, but the reputation of your company is at stake. Stories of badly handled grievances spread like wildfire. Before you know it, you could have half the workforce up in arms, not just Topi!

15

Inappropriate Behaviour

Definition

A conversation to make a person aware that they are acting in a way that is considered inappropriate in the workplace, and to request that they change this specific behaviour.

Outcomes

- You have described the boundaries of acceptable/unacceptable behaviour at work, and explained why this is the case.

- Topi has new understanding about how her behaviour is perceived, and knows what changes are required.

- Both sides are clear what will happen next if the behaviour is not modified.

Think Ahead

- What specifically is the behaviour you want to see changed?

- Why does it need to be changed? Why should Topi change to suit you?

- What impact is the behaviour having on others?

- Weighing up the balance between the impact of Topi's behaviour and productivity, on which side do the scales tip? If Topi wasn't there, would you lose more than you gain? Is the irritation a small price to pay for the eccentricity – or is it more serious than that?

- What should Topi replace the unwanted behaviour with? You need to be able to describe or demonstrate this in detail.

- What support can Topi be given to help her to change?

- If the issue is not addressed what will the outcome be?

Steps

- Firstly, explain to Topi her strengths and worth as an employee.

- Tell her there is an aspect of her behaviour that you need to discuss with her.

- Ask her how she feels this particular behaviour impacts on others. When you discover how self aware she is you will have some clue about how to proceed.

- Gently but firmly describe how the behaviour appears to others and the knock-on impact it has on her work.

- Allow Topi time to come to terms with what you have said. Answer any questions she may have, and provide real examples or evidence if necessary. Allow her to express her emotions if she needs to. Do not let yourself get sidetracked.

- Ask Topi what she thinks she can do differently. If she is stuck, describe for her how you would like to see her act in the workplace.

- Discuss the support Topi will need to make the changes.

- Reiterate again Topi's value to the company. Help her to keep the issue in perspective.

Good Practice

Inappropriate behaviour is a wide subject.

Topi might have a singular aspect of her personality which is causing problems and which needs to be identified quite carefully. This could be something like shouting or swearing, failing to respect diversity, eating aromatic hot food where others are trying to work, leaving a mess, or flirting in a way that makes colleagues feel uncomfortable.

Thin ice

Let's not beat about the bush: we are treading on very thin ice here.

Our individual behaviour is our only way of showing our personality to the world. If someone criticises this, it is very likely to be taken to heart and cause offence. You will need to be very sensitive towards Topi, and remember that personal criticism can cut deeply.

Is it Topi's problem?

We need to be very sure of our ground. Firstly, we need to be very sure that the behaviour is in fact inappropriate and not just disliked by us. Secondly, how can we prove this? Do we have a written policy that is being flouted? Is there a description of the organisation's culture that shows a different way of working? Even if Topi's colleagues are up in arms about her behaviour, there is always the possibility that they are being intolerant and could be more accepting.

Let's assume that you have decided that Topi's behaviour cannot be tolerated and needs to be changed. The next thing you need to think about is this: if you, and most other people, can see that the behaviour causes issues, why can't Topi? You really need to get to the bottom of this to stand a chance of persuading Topi to change.

Possible options are:

- She has never thought about it.

- The way she behaves has been accepted, or even welcomed, in other places she has worked.

- She is indoctrinated because everyone else in her family has always acted in the same way.

- She doesn't like the way she acts, but she has no idea what she could replace the behaviour with.

- She gets pleasure from being different.

- She really doesn't care what you think.

Looking at that list, you could be running scared! How would you respond to each one? It could be complicated, but you have a right to do all you can to make the workplace as productive and harmonious as possible.

Making it better

There is, fortunately, some good news:

- In most instances, Topi really does not want to upset anyone. As soon as she realises she is offending colleagues or alienating customers she could be mortified and change tack rapidly.

- She may want to change, but not know how. Help her in easy steps, and she will be on her way to being a different person.

- Even if, deep down, she doesn't give a hoot about what people think of her, she could still value her job and want to keep it, in which case she will be cooperative.

You will have probably gathered by now that the key to handling the situation effectively is twofold. You need to be in control of your own feelings, and able to handle Topi's reactions. You also need convincing evidence that change would benefit all concerned.

Warning!

- If can take six months to learn new behaviour, and a lot longer to unlearn entrenched behaviour. You may need to be patient.

- Check, double check, then triple check that Topi has absolutely no grounds for claiming that you have harassed her, bullied her, or behaved unreasonably.

16

Influencing and Persuading

Definition

Using your personal power to sway a colleague's behaviour or opinion, in order to further appropriate aims.

Outcomes

- You acquire an ally.

- Topi is happy to go along with your wishes.

Think Ahead

- What is your view on the ethics of consciously trying to make someone behave differently? How does that sit with the culture of your workplace?

- What type of power do you have over this person? (see below)

- How good is your working relationship with Topi? Does she like you? Does she respect you?

- Does Topi have any reason to think that you are worthy of her agreement or support?

- What could you do to strengthen Topi's general opinion of you?

- How are you like Topi? How are you different?

Steps

- Influencing is more of an ongoing process than a structured discussion, so give some thought to your existing relationship with Topi first. This is unlikely to work if you are at loggerheads.

- **Work out which sources of power** and principles of influence will resonate most strongly with Topi.

- **Point out to Topi your common ground** (social proof) and if possible tactfully remind her of times you have supported her (reciprocity).

- **Make your request.** Be straightforward, but do let Topi know how much you would appreciate it, and say what you can do for her in return.

- **If she is reluctant, do not be pushy**. If she senses coercion, she will push back. If you pull rank, she may comply, but that is not as good as having her on your side.

Good Practice

Ethics

Let's start by stating the obvious. It is important that you are aware that using your power at work needs to be done within the context of the values of the organisation and your own personal (and hopefully sound) ethics.

That said, every time we interact with another person we are influencing them somehow. They may decide, through experiencing our behaviour, that they like us, respect us, enjoy being around us... Or possibly they never want to see us again!

Once they have reached a conclusion, it will affect how they behave around us in the future. It is not impossible to influence someone who has no time for you, but it is much easier if you are starting from a position of mutual like and respect.

Making it work

It is also important to take time to get to know Topi. If you have no idea of what drives her, what her passions are and how she likes to operate, you will be groping in the dark when it comes to choosing a tactic to try to win her round - unless you happen to have the charisma of fame, in which case you are in with a chance.

There has been much research into influencing and persuasion that can help us understand how it works. Let's have a brief look at a couple of pieces that are helpful; please read further if you want to know more.

Sources of power

Power is the ability to induce, change or influence what others think, believe and do.

The most common model used is by French and Raven. It identifies five sources of power. As you read through, think about which ones could be applied to your relationship with Topi:

- **Referent power**

  This is personal or emotional power. Others will do as you wish because they gain personal satisfaction from being identified with you. They may respect you, like you, admire your personal qualities, enjoy your company, or aspire to be like you. They are attracted to you like bees to a honey pot, you are worthy of their respect. This is the power of charisma and fame.

- **Expert power**

  Others assume that you have superior skills, abilities, information, knowledge or expertise. For example, when I have knowledge that you want, I have expert power. This is a very common form of power in the workplace, and the basis for most collaboration – but it maybe used in a narrow, specialised field. Doctors and lawyers are good examples of holders of expert power.

- **Legitimate power**

  This is the power of formal rank or position. The power holder has the right to require and demand compliance as they have been granted authority. Your boss or the police are good examples. This source of power works because there is a human tendency to obey authorities. Obedience usually comes much more easily to us than disobedience.

- **Reward power**

  This is the power of being able to give someone more of what they want, or the ability to take away from them the things they don't want. It is about control over valued resources. Others are aware that you can assign grades, offer promotion, or reward them in some other way. Anything others find desirable can be a reward, from a yacht to a pat on the back. Compliments count too.

- **Coercive power**

  This is having the capacity to give out punishments or force someone to do something against their will. This could be relying on physical strength, always being able to win an argument, withholding emotional support, or using humiliation or insults. Using this type of power causes problems and leads to abuse.

What power have you got?

The interesting thing about French and Raven's theory of power is how people respond to the different types. There are no prizes for deducing that if you force Topi against her will, she will resist you as much as she can and you certainly won't win any respect or affection. If you force your hand you may win for the moment, but your relationship is very likely to be damaged in the long term.

If you use reward or legitimate power Topi is probably going to comply with your wishes. However, we don't always have legitimate power, and we may be limited in the rewards we can offer that Topi values.

This leaves us with two sorts of power- referent and expert – which brings some good news. It is these two types of power that actually inspire commitment from others. You can draw your own conclusion, but it is obvious that being likeable and willing to share your knowledge will take you far when it comes to influencing Topi.

So, if you can gain confidence and credibility you can build a platform for persuasion and power.

Principles of influence

Robert Cialdini has carried out extensive research into how influence works, and is famous for identifying six universal principles for influencing. No single principle works all the time, but being aware of them will give you the best chance of success:

- **Reciprocation.** We have a tendency to return favours and pay back debts; we like to give back what has been given to us, even if it is only a smile. The first rule is that Topi is more likely to comply with your request if you have previously done something similar for her, as she may feel obliged to reciprocate. If you have helped her out on a project, she is more likely to volunteer to work late for you.

- **Commitment/Consistency.** People like to look consistent within their words, beliefs, attitudes, and deeds, and this is, on the whole, is valued by society. People are more willing to be moved in a particular direction if they see it as consistent with an existing or recent commitment they have made. The initial commitment can be quite small, for example a giving a little donation to a charity, yet we are still more inclined to give again than if we had not donated before.

- **Authority.** This has echoes of French and Raven's source of legitimate power. People are more willing to follow the directions or recommendations of someone they think has relevant authority or expertise. Studies have shown that we attribute more power and intelligence to a man in a suit and tie than someone more casually dressed. Should we dress for success?

- **Social Proof.** This is 'herd mentality'. We see what other people are doing, and conclude it would be a good idea for us to do it too. People are more willing to take action if they see that others, especially people similar to them, are taking it. You can induce a type of behaviour if you can show that others are doing the same thing.

- **Scarcity.** People find things more attractive if they think they are scarce or about to run out. Think about every time the news says that tanker drivers are on strike, or there is a food shortage – suddenly we are stockpiling as if we could never shop again. Can you add rarity value to the action you're trying to get Topi to take?

- **Liking/Friendship.** Topi prefers to say yes to people she knows and likes. How often do we buy products or services because we are friends with someone? It can actually be quite hard to turn away from a person we like or deny a request. Friendship inspires loyalty.

Which to use?

So, there we have it – several clues that will help us understand how we can win Topi round. Every situation is different; it is up to you to consider which combination of approaches will work best this time. The bottom line appears to be that the better your relationship with Topi, and the more you understand her drivers and interests, the better position you are in to get her on your side.

Warning!

- If you use your power unethically, you will end up with short term gains and long term notoriety.

- Pick your battles carefully. Sometimes it is better to let something go, and save your energy for a situation that is more important.

- If you in the habit of disregarding a person until you want something, you aren't going to win any respect. It will always be an uphill struggle.

Instructing

Definition

Helping another person learn how to carry out a specific task or procedure.

Outcomes

- You have explained the task or procedure in a way that Topi is able to grasp.

- Topi is competent to carry out the task or procedure with minimal or no supervision.

Think Ahead

- How does Topi like to take in information?

- How can you adapt your usual approach to suit his preference?

- Are there written/visual/audio/video instructions Topi can refer to? What would work best?

- Can you find simpler phrases for jargon and technical vocabulary that Topi may struggle with?

- Do you have a basic grasp of how adults learn?

- How will you know when Topi can carry out the task to your - and his - satisfaction?

Steps

- **Check that Topi is ready**, willing and able to absorb new knowledge.

- **Explain to Topi why the instructions are necessary.**

- **Break the task down into small steps.** For each step, demonstrate, or use a visual aid to back up your words. Be clear and specific.

- **Let Topi have a go** at each stage if appropriate.

- **Give Topi an opportunity to ask questions** after each stage, and recap the learning.

- **Build up the learning in logical, consequential steps.** Each step should build on the previous one.

- **Check that Topi understands the instructions.**

- **Find a way** to make sure he has an opportunity to use the instructions and repeat them in the near future.

Good Practice

If your aim is to encourage Topi to be more proactive and solve his own problems, you are probably better off looking at the chapter on coaching. The coaching approach is usually more productive in the long run, but there are times when all we need to do is to teach Topi how to do something new, for example operate a new piece of equipment or follow a procedure.

There is a very wise old Chinese proverb, attributed to Confucius:

"I hear and I forget. I see and I remember. I do and I understand."

The even shorter version is *"Tell, Show, Do"*, which gives us a good basic structure for helping others to learn.

Learning styles

We do not all take information on board in the same way. We may have different learning styles and varying types of ability. Finding out how Topi learns best can make it easier for you to choose a way to pass information to him.

Some of us prefer to take things in by reading, some like to talk things through or listen, others want to watch someone show them how, and some want to dive straight in and learn by doing.

This means that, unless you are very sure of Topi's learning style, it is a good plan to include several different methods of getting your message across.

For example, you might:

- Explain to Topi that you will be using a new computerised system.

- Show him how it works. Give him exact instructions.

- Ask him to have a go with you standing by to guide him if needed.

- Let him view written instructions.

- Let him have a go without your help.

- Discuss with him now the new system will be used, answer questions, and let him come up with ideas for rolling it out.

You will then have covered many learning styles and hopefully will have Topi's preferred style included. Do take note of when he responds easily, and when he struggles, as it will give you valuable clues that you can use another time. There is more about learning styles in the chapter on coaching.

However you instruct Topi, remember to:

- Use language that Topi is familiar with.

- Use diagrams and pictures to supplement your words.

- Back up with easy to follow written instructions. Bulleted lists are simple to review. Numbering can help too.

- Ask Topi to explain it back to you so that you can check if he understands.

- Don't give many instructions at once. Topi will forget.

Warning!

- The message given is not always the same as the message received. Just because you have told someone, you cannot assume they have heard and understood what you meant.

- If Topi does not have the opportunity to use the instructions soon and repeatedly he may forget or become less confident about using them.

- Your natural inclination will be to instruct according to your own learning style, not Topi's. Check yourself!

18

Interviewing Job Applicants

Definition

A formal discussion with an applicant for a job, to assess their suitability for the role.

Outcomes

- You have explored, in a systematic way, Topi's suitability against the requirements of the job you are trying to fill.

- You have reached a conclusion about Topi's suitability, or decided to hold a second interview if you feel you need to probe further.

- Topi feels satisfied that she has had a good opportunity to talk about her skills, experience, and why she thinks she is the right candidate for the job.

- You have created a good impression of the company.

Think Ahead

- Have you defined exactly what the job is? Interviewing is much easier if you have a job description that lists the tasks involved.

- In addition to a job description, do you have a person specification? This describes the person you need to carry out the job. Headings are usually skills, experience, knowledge, and personal attributes. Often they are listed in two columns headed essential and desirable.

- You will need to prepare questions designed to find out if the candidate meets your requirements on every point of the person specification.

- If Topi does not give you a full enough answer, you should have some extra probing questions ready to help you find out more.

- You will need a method of scoring and comparing candidates. Many people use a scale of 1-5.

- Are you up to date with legislation? You will need to know about discrimination and disability. If in doubt, consult an HR professional.

Steps

- **Set Topi at ease,** she will probably be nervous.

- **Explain what is going to happen** and how long the interview to last.

- **Ask the questions you have prepared.** For each one, explore Topi's answer until you feel you have sufficient information to score her suitability on that particular point.

- **Ask Topi if she has any questions for you.**

- **Tell Topi what will happen next**, i.e. when you will make your decision and what the next step will be.

- **Give yourself time to complete your scoring** and make any notes while the interview is fresh in your mind.

Good Practice

Preparation

Many people struggle with hiring new staff - mistakes are made, which can be very costly and time consuming. The secret of success is in preparation: if you have a good set of questions that link to the job description and person specification you should do well. It takes time, but will save you much more bother in the long run.

Also consider the environment. You're in control of the situation, so choose a room where you won't be disturbed and can create the right mood. Most people conduct a formal interview from behind a desk to maintain an objective, professional distance, although this can cause Topi to clam up. If you want to find out if Topi would work well with you try sitting at 90 degrees to her to create a more collaborative approach to matching each other's needs.

Is she a STAR?

Questions should give Topi an opportunity to tell stories that give examples of her competence and experience. One popular approach is asking for STAR stories. STAR stands for

• Situation

• Task

• Action

• Result

Say, for example, you want to know how Topi handles customer complaints. You might ask her to tell you about a former position in retail (situation), when a customer complained (task), how she dealt with the complaint (action), and what the outcome was (result).

Go with gut instinct?

Sometimes you will hear someone say that their gut instinct tells them instantly if a candidate is the right person. If you have a vast amount of interview experience it is possible that your instinct may well be good.

However, even if you're sure you must still give all candidates an equal opportunity to present their case at interview. You may find that first impressions are not always right.

You could also save yourself from a lawsuit; if a disgruntled candidate complained that you had not treated him fairly, you may have to provide evidence that you chose the best person for the job. *"My gut told me"* might not impress a judge!

Beware of false impressions

Another thing to be wary of is the halos and horns phenomenon. If Topi says something that impresses us (halo) or something we disapprove of (horns) it is easy to jump to a conclusion, and only hear further evidence that backs up our initial conclusion.

It is important that we postpone judgement and remain impartial until we have carefully gathered all the evidence available. The danger is that you could overlook a major flaw in Ms Halo, or write off Mr Horns when actually he is overall the best of the candidates.

Preconceived ideas

Another way of skewing judgement is to have a fixed preconception of what the right candidate will look like. This in fact is a form of prejudice. When you visualise the perfect person for the job, what do you see? How rigid are your thoughts? Try to leave your bias outside the door.

Pace yourself

One last tip – don't do too many interviews in a row. The level of concentration required to listen well makes interviewing hard work, and also there is a limit to what you will remember.

Allow time to make notes as fully as you can between candidates, because by the end of a busy day there is every chance that you will have forgotten the first person you interviewed. Some interviewers even staple a photo to the notes to help them remember.

Create a good impression

So far, we have only considered finding out about Topi – but Topi will also want to find out about you, too. Part of the role of the interviewer is to project an image of the organisation you represent, to help the candidates decide if they would like to work for you.

Consider the environment from Topi's viewpoint. Does it reflect your company well? Is it sufficiently business like? Will it be free from distractions, so that you can concentrate on the job at hand? And does it reflect the culture of your business honestly and positively?

Warning!

- If you break the law and do not treat candidates fairly, they can take you to a tribunal. Make sure you are fully aware of the relevant legislation.

- Your candidate seemed perfect – but was she truthful? Do take up references to back up your findings.

- Is the best candidate good enough? You may be desperate to get someone in place, but it is a false economy to cross your fingers and hope that that a weak candidate will do a good job.

Managing Your Boss

Definition

Having a discussion with the purpose of making sure your boss hears your voice and takes your views on board.

Outcomes

- You have a better understanding of how your boss makes decisions, reaches conclusions, and the key factors that influence him.

- Your boss reviews his opinions to take yours into account.

- You have had an opportunity to express yourself firmly and fairly.

Think Ahead

- What do you already know about how your boss operates?

- Looking back at the character descriptions from The Basics at the beginning of this book, how would you describe your boss's personality?

- How could you adapt your style to maximise the chance that your boss will hear and understand?

- What holds you back from being open and honest with your boss?

- What is it that you want to say to your boss?

- Why do you want to say it? What is the worst that could happen if you do say it?

- What would the result be if you held your tongue and said nothing?

- What hard facts and evidence do you have to back up your position?

- If it is a problem that you need to discuss with your boss, what ideas do you have for a solution?

- How would you see things if you were in his shoes?

- Can you describe, as specifically as you can, what it is you want your boss to do?

Steps

- **Arrange a time** to talk with your boss, using the opportunity to reinforce the purpose of the meeting, i.e. you have an idea to discuss, you need support with a project etc. Try not to use language that will alienate your boss before she gets there, and set a positive tone if you can.

- **Get to the point** because bosses rarely have time to waste. Summarise what you want to discuss, and what you want from your boss

- **Ask the boss what her views are on the topic at hand.** This will help you gauge her knowledge and views on the subject.

- **Reiterate common ground;** make it obvious you are both on the same side.

- **State clearly how you see the situation,** how it is affecting you and your work, and what you would like to happen.

- **Listen to what your boss has to say,** without getting defensive. Explore her viewpoint until you can see it from her point of view.

- **Review your starting position if necessary -** or restate it!

- **Agree a time for a follow up discussion** or decision if appropriate. Some people do not like being put on the spot, so you could give your boss some time to think about your thoughts.

Good Practice

Managing upwards

Too often we expect our bosses to have the answers, or we expect them to take all responsibility for problem solving. *"It's not my job to think!"* is an appallingly short sighted approach for you to take to managing your own career. It may seem reasonable just to follow your boss's instructions – after all they do get paid more than you - but if you take the initiative to communicate with them more effectively, or see what you can contribute to help them do their own job well, there are likely to be substantial pay offs for you in terms of getting your own needs met and your voice heard.

Getting the result you want

Bear in mind that promotion decisions are often based on exposure. You may do a brilliant job, but if you keep a low profile it is all too easy to be passed over when opportunities arise. Regular, positive interactions with your boss – or anyone in a higher position - will keep you and your skills in sharp focus.

To do this, you will need a combination of skills. You may want to read up on assertiveness techniques to help you speak confidently; the chapter on influencing might give you some tips too.

The bottom line is that you need to be able to talk your boss's language, see things through their eyes, and stand your ground when you need to. You may have a different job role to your boss, but that does not alter the fact that you are entitled to your opinions and to be heard.

To manage your boss you should:

- Make sure you understand the bigger picture, so that you can see the context that your communication is received in. What direction is the company going in? What pressure is your boss under?

- Find out what style of communication your boss prefers and use it. Note the effectiveness of different types of communication on outcomes.

- Avoid swamping those above you with information. Your case will be much more effective if you limit your input to short, sharp, relevant facts in plain language. If you overload your boss, your message will get lost or diluted. Try and distil it down to key information.

- Present your business case taking the boss's viewpoint into account. Make your thinking explicit, so that she can judge for herself if you are being reasonable, analytical and thoughtful.

- Propose possible solutions and a range of options with your problems. Know which of the options is your preferred solution, and why.

- Be open, honest and direct when giving your boss feedback, the same as you would for your team members. They are not mind readers and may not realise the effect their management style or action is having on you or your team.

- Make sure you have done your homework if you are delegating upwards, so that you can answer any query. You will need a convincing case for the work being your boss's obligation, not yours.

- Offer your support or find a way to bridge the gap if you have a strength where your boss is weak. Bosses have weaknesses too; none of us are perfect. In addition to earning brownie points by making her life easier, there is likely to be wider positive impact on the team around you.

- Keep lines of communication open. Sometimes managers pigeonhole staff and do not realise that they have drawn an incorrect conclusion, or failed to notice we have changed. It is in your best interests to make sure that your boss has an accurate perception of you.

Warning!

- If there is something about your boss's manner or behaviour that stops you communicating openly with them, do you need to address that issue first?

- A common mistake is to bottle up the problems until you go in all guns blazing! Remember that you can always increase the level of muscle you use, but it is very hard to undo the damage caused by acting like a sledgehammer.

20
Mentoring

Definition

A relationship between Topi and a more experienced person, where the more experienced person acts as a trusted adviser: challenging, listening and supporting Topi to help her develop her career and life skills, make choices and decide on ways forward.

Outcomes

- Topi grows in confidence and in her own ability to solve her problems and make wise decisions.

- You grow in your experience of developing others, which may include using skills such advising, coaching or counselling.

Think Ahead

- Why are you doing this? What are your motives? What is in it for you?

- Do you have the time and commitment to be a mentor?

- What ground rules do you want in place e.g. length and frequency of meetings, arrangements for other ad hoc contact, confidentiality?

- What skills may you need to develop?

- Are you confident that you can challenge? Get to the heart of the matter? Help Topi generate options and solutions?

- What will you do if you find yourself out of your depth?

Steps

For the first meeting:

- **Introduce yourself** and set Topi at ease.

- **Briefly share your experience or background** if you do not know each other well.

- **Ask Topi what she understands about mentoring,** and what she expects from you.

- **Correct any misconceptions**, or discuss any differing perceptions.

- **Discuss the practicalities of how it will work** such as ground rules, boundaries, when and where to meet.

- **Ask Topi what she would like to discuss,** and what she hopes to achieve through having a mentor.

- **Prioritise the issues** if she has many, so that you have an agenda that reflects what is most important to her.

- **Show interest in Topi's work life**, to help you understand how the issues fit in to the bigger picture.

- **Agree what happens next**. Don't be afraid to ask Topi to do work between sessions, e.g. research, or raising concerns with others.

Good Practice

A good start

Mentoring is not a one off meeting, but rather a series of discussions where Topi brings the agenda. Above you will find the important points to cover in the first meeting. These are around getting to know Topi and her ambitions, but also setting the scene so that she has an accurate understanding of what to expect from you.

Most of the things that go wrong with mentoring relationships are because this initial agreement was not done, and one person had unrealistic expectations. Topi may bring the topics to the table, but you have responsibility for managing the relationship.

As well as agreeing how you will work together, the other thing to consider is your personal style. If you were in Topi's shoes and you wanted to share a problem or talk through an issue with someone, how would you choose who to approach? What is it about this person that attracts your confidence?

Another definition of a mentor is *"a wise, trusted friend"*. It means:

- Having regular contact and building trust

- Providing support and encouragement

- Helping Topi find a way through her problems

- Giving Topi your knowledge and experience when appropriate.

Does that sound like you?

Attributes of an Effective Mentor

Mentoring relationships vary and may require different skills and behaviours depending on the needs of the mentee. It is not for everyone – some people are just not cut out to be mentors.

Good mentors have a range of attributes. How do you measure up?

- **Able to build rapport** and avoid rapport-breaking behaviour.

- **Self aware,** recognising impact of self on others, knowing own strengths and weaknesses.

- **Genuine**, open and honest, willing to share experience appropriately.

- **Patient**, and able to pace to meet Topi's needs, reaching conclusions at the right time.

- **Positive,** encouraging, and able to give praise, recognition and respect. Making Topi feel valued, accepted and appreciated.

- **Non judgmental**/open minded. Able to accept and work with differing beliefs, values, cultures.

- **Supportive.** Able to empathise, demonstrate understanding.

- **Interested in people**, development of self and others.

- **Able to explain**/communicate clearly. Able to use appropriate language, level of detail.

- **Able to listen,** and to give full attention and draw out full understanding.

- **Questioning**/reflecting/summarising.

- **Good at problem solving.** Lateral thinking, creative approach, ability to view obstacles as movable.

- **Resilient**. Does not become overly anxious about the mentee's problems or pass own stress on.

- **Proficient in learning and development**. Aware of different learning styles, learning cycles (see the chapter on Coaching).

- **Willing to challenge sensitively** and appropriately.

A mentoring meeting does not necessarily have a structure, as you may not know in advance how Topi wants to use her time with you. She may need your assistance to be able to see the big picture, understand the politics of the organisation you work for, or get guidance on how to progress her career.

As long as it is meaningful and productive, you will have done well. Mentoring should encourage learning and improved performance.

A powerful framework

Gerard Egan's model from The Skilled Helper may help you to structure a discussion. He describes three stages:

- **Where are you now?** Listening and questioning until you understand as fully as possible,

- **Where are you going?** Exploring options and possibilities, viewing the situation from different angles, discussing pros and cons.

- **How will you get there?** Help Topi decide which is the best way forward, setting practical goals and action points.

These stages are described in more detail, and in a non academic way, in The One to One Toolkit (Cooper and Reynolds)

What should you be doing?

When you're engaging with Topi you should be meeting her needs, but make sure you're also:

- **Exploring the issue.** Mentors make good sounding boards, but Topi may be reticent to reveal her real issues. Express your genuine interest, and learn to ask probing questions to find out the full picture, e.g. *"What makes you say that?"*, *"Tell me more about that"*, *"How did that come about?"*.

- **Generating and exploring options** is also important. Help Topi think about how she could behave differently, or use a different approach. Guiding her to see things from another person's perspective can be useful.

- **Encouraging.** Offer sufficient praise and recognition to help Topi feel valued and respected, particularly if your conversation has been focused on problems and difficulties. Make sure Topi can see for herself what she has achieved, and how she has done it. Mentoring often involves helping Topi see the wood for the trees!

- **Clarifying outcomes.** Summarising a discussion will ensure that both of you are clear about what has been discussed and agreed. If your meeting results in action points, note them using language that is meaningful to Topi.

- **Record keeping.** It can be helpful to jot brief notes to remind you both of what you have discussed, what actions you've agreed, and what you want to cover next time. Where possible, do this before the end of the meeting; it will help build trust if your record keeping is transparent.

When you reach your limits

One of the boundaries you need to be aware of is your own competence. You are probably not a trained counsellor, nurse or psychologist. If Topi has needs that you cannot meet, you should discuss an appropriate referral with her. Make it your responsibility to find out how she can access the help she needs.

If it is more a case of the relationship just being stuck in a rut, here are some tips:

- Persevere – it can take several meetings before Topi has sufficient trust to open up.

- See what variables you can change – venue, pace, activity, length of meeting etc.

- Read up on some brainstorming or lateral thinking techniques to get things moving (e.g. De Bono's Thinking Course).

A mentoring relationship should be mutually beneficial. If you really cannot get on with Topi, and you feel that she is not benefiting from the sessions at all, it may be best to withdraw from the relationship and suggest a new mentor is found.

What is the difference between coaching and mentoring?

You may be wondering what the difference is between mentoring and coaching; there are many definitions of both, and both use many of the same skills.

Mentoring usually takes a broader perspective, taking into account career aspirations, and offering personal or emotional support. It tends to be a deeper relationship based on trust and mutual respect, and is concerned more with developing a protégé to reach their full potential than with helping a co-worker to brush up their skills.

Someone outside line management usually carries out mentoring, although there may be times when a line manager finds himself in conversations that are best described as mentoring.

If you are being mentored

The best approach is to use someone who can be more objective and impartial than your line manager who, after all, has a vested interest in how you do your job. Would you really be willing to discuss your escape plan with your boss?

Take responsibility for making sure that your time with your mentor is fruitful. You can best achieve this by thinking in advance what your priorities are, and what specifically you would like your mentor to help you with. Do not use him as a dumping ground.

You may want to review how you have handled situations in the past, but do make sure that you also look forward so that learning can be applied. You will also need to be able to handle feedback, be willing to be honest about your development needs, and be prepared to be challenged.

Warning!

- Topi may well be able to benefit from your experience, but don't assume that telling her how you lived your life will be of any use to her. Share your experience when she wants to hear it, not when you want to tell it.

- Don't belittle Topi's problems. We all assign different values and weights to our issues – what is trivial to you may seem like a mountain to climb to Topi. Help her see it in perspective by all means, but be careful not to mock.

- Don't assume Topi shares your values and interests just because she works for the same organisation. She may not.

21

Negotiating

Definition

Any discussion where two people seek to reach agreement from different starting positions.

Outcomes

- Both sides have expressed their needs, wants, and flexibility.

- An agreement is reached that is acceptable to both parties.

Think Ahead

- What is it you are trying to achieve? What is at stake?

- Get as much background information as you can about the Topi's position and what he might want.

- How much you are prepared to compromise? What are the repercussions if you do?

- Do a risk/benefit analysis. This means weighing up what you could gain against what you could lose. Assessing the strengths and weaknesses of both sides is part of this process.

- Be clear about your parameters. It is not wise to reveal these to Topi, but you will need to know the bottom line on costs, timescales, availability, etc.

- Identify your objectives. If you have several, prioritise them. You may need to lose the battle to win the war.

Steps

- **Establish rapport,** for example safe small talk, suitable language, etc.

- **Opening phase.** This is when both sides share their basic interests, but not the specifics.

- **Test your assumptions** about Topi's interests before you act on them. Wrong assumptions are one of the most common hazards.

- **Gather information.** Explore issues, e.g. urgency, importance, other factors involved.

- **Establish the ground rules.** E.g. how much time you have, deadlines, conditions, relevant company policy, etc.

- **Discuss the issues.** This stage may take longer than you expect. If you seem to be making no progress, try to clarify the points you agree on and those that still need to be settled.

- **Reach agreement/make decisions.** Clarification is all-important here. Devise a checklist for who is doing what, when, agreed costs, timescales, etc. Confirm in writing.

- **Close.** Once a deal has been struck, it is usually good practice to end the conversation fairly swiftly. Always make sure that you end on a positive note.

Good Practice

Often you might shy away from situations where negotiation is needed, because you perceive it as conflict. Of course,your fears have some grounds, as a negotiation is about dealing with opposing positions. Some people use what is called the 'hard' approach, and view Topi as the enemy, distrust her, apply pressure and want to win at all costs.

The opposite approach is 'soft', wanting to avoid conflict at all costs, giving in to Topi in an attempt to keep the peace. Neither extreme is ideal: both approaches can lead to damaged relationships, such as feelings of being exploited or not trusted in the future. Fortunately, there is an alternative.

Principled negotiation

The Harvard Negotiation Project, (described by Fisher and Ury) gives us a model that aims to *"produce wise outcomes efficiently and amicably"*, which finds a different path by being hard on the problem but soft on the people involved. It has four key principles:

- **People**. Separating the person from the problem is not a new concept, but has not always been applied to negotiation situations. Participants should see themselves as working alongside the other side, as two parties trying to solve the problem, as opposed to taking opposite sides and attacking each other. Emotions often become tangled with positions: people have feelings, values and background which may help or hinder the negotiation. See the negotiation of consisting of two parts – the relationship and the subject under discussion.

- **Interests**. Focus on Topi's interests, not her position. What are the desires and concerns that are leading to the position being stated? If attention is paid to Topi's position, less attention is given to her underlying concerns and interests. Positional bargaining is also more likely to degenerate into a battle of wills. Look behind positions for shared interests that you can reconcile and agree.

- **Options**. Generate a variety of options before deciding what to do. Again, not a new idea, but usually only applied to creative problem solving where only one party or group is involved. Take time out to do this between you if you can.

- **Criteria**. Use objective criteria to reach an outcome based on independent standards rather than personal preference. This will produce a fairer solution. Be open to reason about what standards should be applied. The criteria might come from company policy, for example, or average prices, standards of good practice from professional bodies, or previous research.

Paying attention to these four principles will give you the best chance of coming up with a solution that is fair to both sides. The 'Three-Step Tango' in The Basics section may also be useful.

Win/win negotiation

Another phrase you will have heard is win/win. Here are a few tips that will help both sides feel that neither has lost:

- You are two professionals looking for a common solution. One of you has a problem; the other may have the answer.

- Identify common ground that you both agree upon.

- Remain pleasant and control your behaviour when the going gets tough. If you cannot achieve this, postpone until you have calmed down. Blowing your stack rarely leads to success.

- Do not make proposals until both sides are clear about the situation. Premature solutions often go pear shaped, so set realistic timescales. Using tentative proposals can help you to identify the gap between you.

- If your proposal is not accepted, or you are rejecting Topi's proposal, repeat your common ground, mutual benefits etc to help maintain a positive working environment. You may need to agree to differ, or to compromise.

Strategies

There are many books on negotiation strategies, but some will not sit comfortably with principled negotiation, and may challenge your own ethics and values. You will need to use your sense of fairness and your conscience when choosing which strategies to use, and also take the context into account. Here a few of the sounder ones for consideration:

- Resolve the small issues first. This will establish good faith.

- If you are not sure how responsive or flexible Topi is willing to be, try a trial request; ask for something unimportant or minor, and see how she responds.

- Let the other side make the first offer; usually the first offer is the starting point for negotiation, so if you make it, it is your position that starts to be eroded.

- Suggest splitting the difference (if you do this twice the right way round, you get 75%of the difference!).

- If you really cannot make any progress with the other side, and you have tried every strategy you can think of, it might be about differences in personal style. Get a colleague to take over.

- If you are at stalemate, brainstorming with the other side may get things moving again. This means coming up with ideas, without stopping to evaluate them. Often among the unusable there will be a seed of an idea that can be used to come up with a different approach to a solution. If you use this, make sure both sides understand what is going on, so that brainstorming does not get confused with decision making.

- Yes, yes, yes...get the other side to say *"yes"* a few times to create a positive environment.

- Think about closure from the beginning; know what a successful outcome will look like, and what the best alternative is.

Dealing with underhand tactics

Sometimes, and hopefully it is rarely, you may come across someone who uses dirty tricks when negotiating. They may lie, mislead or bully you in an attempt to get their own way. Your best defence is to take an open, honest stance rather than ignoring it.

Once you have recognised it, raise the issue overtly and unambiguously with Topi and then question the use of the tactic during the negotiation. This gives you the opportunity to negotiate the rules of the game. Often, just letting it be known that you are aware of Topi's strategy will be enough to diffuse the situation. Do not become a victim; remain objective and defend yourself by adhering to your own values and principles.

Closing strategies

Sales people are trained in a whole raft of closing techniques, most of which you have probably encountered. As a principled negotiator, there are probably several that you will not want to try (e.g. intimidating or seeking pity)!

Also bear in mind that decisions are not always rational; people like to do business with people they like, or who brighten their day – so if you can remain pleasant and principled, you will have it cracked. Also ensure that you keep your promises.

An effective close will:

- Summarise the agreement.

- Leave the other side wanting to do business with you again.

- Be reasonably swift. Do not let the conversation ramble on once you reach agreement.

Here are some strategies that can be used at the end of a negotiation:

- **Assume** that Topi has agreed with your proposal and start talking about when and how it is going to happen, rather than if it is going to happen. This is not entirely ethical, but may be appropriate if Topi appears disorganised or incapable of reaching a decision.

- **Be direct.** If you have discussed all the options, put your cards on the table, e.g. *"the very best I can do for you is…"* and wait for a reply.

- **Summarise the benefits/solutions that you can offer.** Benefits and solutions are what people are looking for. Reminding the other side of how your offer will help them can bring the focus you need to close.

- **Offer a temporary or trial solution.** If Topi is concerned about the level of commitment required, offer an option that gives them a get out clause.

- **Offer choices.** Either/or works well. If you offer too many choices, you may confuse Topi, so explain carefully and check that the she understands each one.

Ask!

One of the most fundamental mistakes we make is to assume that others know what we want or need. If we follow the ethics of principled negotiation, which require us to really understand Topi's interests and to make our requirements crystal clear and unmistakeable, effective negotiation can be summed up in five words, one syllable each: **Be on their side. Ask.**

Warning!

- Pick your battles carefully and think of the bigger picture. It is easy to get carried away in our quest to win, but if we need Topi's goodwill further down the line for more important issues, it is worth giving in on the small things.

- Don't let the urge to reach a conclusion overshadow good reasoning. Fast work is sometimes the slowest way of getting things done!

22

Performance Gaps

Definition

A discussion to understand why Topi's work performance has fallen below the expected standard, and to work out how to rectify the situation.

Outcomes

- You have better understanding of the reasons behind Topi's poor performance.

- Topi has a clearer understanding of the standard of work expected from him.

- Action is agreed to help Topi improve his performance.

- Ways of monitoring Topi's progress are agreed.

Think Ahead

- How does Topi know what work is expected of him? Where is this documented? What feedback has he had already?

- What is the evidence that Topi is not performing well?

- Is this a temporary or long term problem? Has Topi performed well in the past?

- Is Topi capable of meeting the standard? What evidence do you have?

- What reasons do you think there might be behind the poor performance?

- What ideas do you have for helping Topi improve his performance?

- Could Topi's job role be modified to better suit his skills?

- What will the repercussions be if Topi cannot or will not meet the standard?

Steps

- **Set the scene**. Explain to Topi that there is an aspect of his performance that you want to discuss.

- **Ask Topi how he thinks he is doing on this aspect of his performance**. Listen carefully to his response; you may pick up clues that will help you find a solution, or discover that he has misunderstood what is expected of him.

- **Explain the expected standard clearly,** and how Topi is falling short. Describe the impact it has. Make sure Topi is clear about the gap between the expected standard and his performance. A useful phrase is *"What I expected was..... What I saw was......"*

- **Ask Topi for his views**. Has he any ideas, development needs or an explanation? You will need to understand the reasons why the performance is below standard before you can make suggestions or plan what to do. Withhold your judgement until you understand it from Topi's viewpoint.

- **Discuss and agree the best way forward**, taking Topi's explanation into account.

- **Arrange a review**, or agree how you will monitor Topi's performance.

Good Practice

The start of any successful challenge to performance gaps is working out how they have come about. Topi's poor performance could be because of organisational issues, personal characteristics or how he relates to others around him. If you reach the wrong conclusion you will have the wrong conversation with Topi, which isn't going to help the situation.

It could be organisational issues...

Think through the following list of factors. Could they be contributing to Topi's poor performance?

- Is his work well planned?

- Is his pay right for his role?

- Does he have the right equipment, in good working order?

- Has he had appropriate training or coaching?

- Has he had time to learn the role, or had changes to cope with?

- Are the physical conditions of the workplace conducive to good performance?

- What distractions are there in the workplace?

- Is he being effectively managed? Does the management system work?

...it could be personal issues

Alternatively, could there be an issue relating to Topi or how he gets on with those around him:

- Is there evidence that Topi has the intellectual capability to do the job?

- Does he appear emotionally stable?

- Does he have any health problems?

- Does he have any domestic difficulties, e.g. childcare, marriage break up?

- Does he fit in with the team?

- Is there a personality clash?

- Is he over or under confident?

- Does the work role conflict with his personal beliefs or values?

- Is he dissatisfied for some reason?

Get it sorted

Before you meet with Topi try to identify likely contributing factors, and think through which of these could be improved or adapted. Organisational issues may be in within your control but, of course, issues personal to Topi probably are not. If you discover that Topi has personal problems you could find out if there are outside agencies that can offer advice or support.

So, you have tried to get to the heart of the matter – but the bottom line is that there is a performance gap that is having an impact on productivity. Thought needs to be given to how you approach the meeting:

- if you are too soft, it will seem like a counselling session and may give Topi the impression that it's acceptable to underperform.

- on the other hand if you are hard on him you will alienate him and move towards conflict. There is evidence that workers perform better when they have a strong relationship with the manager, so maintaining or improving the relationship between you should be one of your aims.

Even though you have analysed the situation before meeting Topi, it is a good move to try to get him to come up with solutions. It is not always possible, but you are more like to get buy in and commitment if you do.

Lateness

One aspect of under performance is lateness – Topi simply isn't around for the full working day. There is one school of thought that says that if Topi is otherwise an exceptional employee, and there is no real reason why he has to be there at a specific time, then leave well alone.

On the other hand, it is more likely that Topi's productivity will be affected by lateness. Much of the advice above still applies. A policy outlining the required standard of timekeeping and consequences will make your position clear. If you don't have one, an HR professional can help you draw one up.

Depending on the cause of the lateness and the nature of your business, you could consider offering Topi a flexible working arrangement, such as staggered hours or temporary home working. It is important to be fair and reasonable – we all occasionally have a problem getting to work.

Like absence, the evidence shows that lateness improves if Topi knows his attendance is being monitored, so make sure he knows that it is being noted.

If Topi doesn't seem aware of the impact of his lateness you could help him understand by pointing out that being ten minutes late every day equates to you giving him a free week's holiday a year! You can also help him realise that he is letting his colleagues down by flouting the rules, while they obey them.

Cause – and effective action

The action you adopt will depend on the causes; which is right in your case?

- **If Topi does not know what is expected of him:**

    Set clear objectives, check that his job description is clear, and ensure that instructions and procedures are understandable and accessible.

- **If Topi did not know that he was not meeting expectations:**

  Ensure he understands the performance gap, arrange to review his work, and give him regular feedback so that he knows how he is doing.

- **If Topi cannot meet expectations:**

  Topi may have learning and development needs, insufficient resources, unrealistic targets, or just not be capable of doing the job. You could arrange training or coaching, a workplace buddy or a mentor. You will need to make him aware that he may lose his job or have his work role changed if all else fails.

- **If Topi will not meet expectations:**

  This can be the hardest issue to deal with, but fortunately it is also the rarest. If Topi appears to have no motivation or an attitude problem you may have no choice but to start formal disciplinary proceedings – which is why it is so important to gather real evidence.

Warning!

- Check your own emotional state. If you bring your own anxiety to the meeting it will be hard to get Topi to open up and be honest. It will also impede your chance to develop a healthy relationship with him.

- No one likes difficult meetings, and a common fault is to try to get out as soon as possible. Allow enough time. It may take longer than you think to unravel the reasons you need to address and to discuss solutions.

23

Praising

Definition

Taking the opportunity to tell a colleague that they have done something well, and the positive impact their action has had on you or others.

Outcomes

- Topi is aware of what she does well, which will make it easier for her to repeat it.

- Topi feels more motivated and engaged with her work.

- You get the feel good factor of noticing the good things, and not just the problems.

Think Ahead

- Who do you appreciate in the workplace? Why?

- How often do you take the time to praise others?

- When do you normally praise others? Could you vary your habits?

- How specific are you in your praise? Do you mention the difference Topi has made?

- What difference do you think it would make to your working relationships if you praised more often?

- How could you notice people doing something right more often?

Steps

- Notice Topi doing something well.

- Think what difference her action has made, and what the outcome could have been if she had acted differently.

- Find an opportunity to tell her you have noticed, and thank her. Be specific about what actions have yielded the results you are pleased with.

Good Practice

Praising is a small thing with a big impact. Most of us know the theory, and yet it is often underused or given cursory attention. Some of us appreciate praise more than others, but you would be hard pushed to find anyone who doesn't value it at all.

Praise breeds success

Maslow's work in the 1940s, which has stood the test of time, identified that we all need a sense of belonging, to be respected, and to feel that we have achieved. This implies that specific praise will help us achieve this. Kenneth Blanchard, in the multimillion selling 'The One Minute Manager', says that praise is not just beneficial, it's critical to success.

Recent work on employee engagement tells the same story. It's been shown that staff turnover is lower, retention is better because people have a sense of attachment to their company, and staff are more motivated to do a better job when *"they feel respected, involved, heard, well led and valued by those they work with"'* (Macleod).

Of course, praising is only one aspect of making Topi feel valued and respected, but it links very well with both helping her to build on her strengths, and building a good relationship with you.

Worthy of praise?

Take a broad view of what makes praiseworthy performance. Your company may be demanding more of people for less, resources and training have been cut back, managers have less time to supervise and support. Sometimes Topi should be praised just for maintaining her output or standards; simply keeping the status quo can be an achievement these days.

Giving effective praise

For praise to work as well as possible:

- Use clear, descriptive language to explain what you are praising and why.

- Make it specific, giving examples or instances.

- Do it very soon after the event that is praiseworthy. For example, saying *"you handled that customer well"* when Topi has spoken to twenty since, will not help her understand what she does well.

- Don't make it a habit – if you only praise at a certain time, or after a regular meeting, your colleagues may not value it as much.

Warning!

- If you praise everything and everyone, you will devalue the praise and lessen its impact.

- Many of us expect a piece of criticism to follow praise, which leads us to skip over it and wait for the negative part. It is ok, when reviewing someone's work, to discuss the good and the bad, but don't let that be you only way of praising. Let praise stand alone where you can.

- Superficial praise can seem patronising. Use concrete examples so that your good intentions are not seen as glib.

- Check your tone to make sure you haven't slipped into parent mode.

24

Making Someone Redundant

Definition

Telling an employee that the company no longer has a need for the role they were employed to do, and therefore their employment will be ended.

Outcomes

- You have explained the redundancy clearly, in a manner that is appropriate, taking Topi's personality into account.

- Next steps, notice period, timescales and any other essential information are given to Topi.

- Topi understands and accepts what needs to happen.

- Topi's initial reaction to the news has been acknowledged and understood.

Think Ahead

- You are legally required to have a period of consultation, so there needs to be a process involving at least two meetings.

- This will almost certainly be difficult news for Topi to hear. Given Topi's personality, how do you think he will respond to the news?

- Given Topi's personal circumstances and skillset, how big a setback is this to him?

- What ongoing support and advice on his next steps will Topi be offered?

- Have the details of the redundancy been prepared in writing for the final meeting. Emotions fog our thinking process, so Topi may not take on board all that you say.

- Tone is especially important when giving bad news. Practise saying what you need to in a calm, clear manner.

- Find out what support is on offer locally outside the company. There may be job clubs or recruitment agencies.

- Investigate if there any is government funding available to help pay for support.

Steps

- **Set the scene,** for example: *"Topi, you will be aware from our previous conversation that the company has had to restructure, and that some roles are to be made redundant"*.

- **Tell Topi calmly and clearly that his role is affected** and that his position is ending.

- **Allow space for Topi to express his emotions**. He may have a lot to say, or he may want to leave the room right away.

- **Acknowledge his feelings** *"I can see you are disappointed...."*

- **Let Topi know what support is on offer** (if any) and what the next steps are.

- **Ask if he has any questions.**

- **Close the meeting, but be sensitive to Topi's needs** and allow space for him to continue talking if he needs it.

Good Practice

You must prepare

Carrying out a redundancy will require at least two meetings.

As mentioned, the first will give Topi notice that redundancies are being considered, and that his role may be affected. You can assure him that you will look at all options. It also gives Topi the chance to contribute any ideas he may have, and tell you anything he feels you should take into account when making your final decision.

Remember that this is a book about conversations, not employment law. We'll assume that you are up to speed with the legalities involved, that you know that there needs to be a period of consultation, and that it is the job role that becomes redundant, not the person. To protect yourself please do make sure that you have all of this thoroughly researched, and that you've talked to an HR professional before you begin the process. This will protect you from claims of unfair dismissal or discrimination.

How not to do it

You have probably heard horror stories about how people have been told about their redundancy – coming to work and finding their desks cleared, getting a text at the weekend, an abrupt meeting ordering them to leave the premises immediately. Of course, it is necessary to protect the employer from potential breaches of confidentiality, but it can cause immeasurable harm to you and your company's reputation if you handle it badly.

Most of the time, there is no escaping the fact that telling someone they are redundant is delivering bad news, even if you have prepared the ground. Most of us shy away from any difficult interaction, using our inbuilt 'fight of flight' mechanism to protect ourselves. This is probably why the horror stories abound – bosses hate dealing with it, because it stirs up negative emotions in them too, so they take the flight option, dropping the news and then running away as soon as possible.

Of course, Topi knows there is a risk that redundancy may be coming. It can still be a shock though, and is near the top of difficult things to deal with in life after bereavement and divorce. If Topi has been in his role a long time, you are effectively taking away a large part of his life and comfort zone.

Managing anxiety

We have already established that there are two sets of anxiety in the meeting – yours, and Topi's. As the person who has instigated the meeting, it is up to you to be responsible for your own emotions – it is not fair for Topi to have to deal with your worries when he has enough of his own.

Think about how your own anxieties will affect the conversation, and what you can do to limit the impact. We have already mentioned fight or flight responses; other potential harm done by our own emotions might include:

- Pussyfooting around the subject, trying to sugar coat or minimise it.

- Being so grave and serious that we make it worse.

- Over compensating by being jolly and gung ho.

- Turning into a sympathetic parent, treating Topi like a child with a grazed knee.

When delivering difficult messages, John Heron talks about *"Telling the truth with love and without compromise"*. You might want to replace *"love"* with *"respect"*, but the general principle is sound – if you are straight with Topi, and also compassionate, you will have done the best job you can.

Of course, it is possible that Topi disliked his job, saw the writing on the wall, and by the time the formal meeting comes he has gleefully planned out the rest of his life and is quite happy. However, it is better to plan for the worst and be pleasantly surprised than the other way round.

Warning!

- Many industries are small pools. News of how you treated Topi will probably get around, be it good or bad. You may even come across Topi again in a couple of years. If you have an 'Out of sight, out of mind' mentality to getting bad news out of the way as quickly as possible, it could come back to haunt you.

- News of handling a redundancy badly travels much, much faster than news of it going smoothly. Add in Chinese whispers, and you have a recipe for your character assassination.

25

Return to Work Interviews

Definition

An interview with an employee who is returning from work after a period of absence.

The purpose is to ensure that Topi's welfare is safeguarded, and the employer is fully briefed with the facts so that he can act accordingly.

Outcomes

- Topi has been welcomed back to work, and any fears or anxieties about returning are discussed and allayed as far as possible.

- If there are any ongoing health issues, the potential impact has been discussed and amendments made to the work area are agreed if appropriate.

- Underlying reasons for absence have been explored.

- Topi is made aware that his absences are noticed and monitored.

Think Ahead

- Gather all the facts – length of absence, content of medical notes etc.

- Arrange a quiet venue.

- Plan some questions, making sure they are not leading, to help you discover how Topi really is.

- Consider whether Topi may have an ongoing health issue. If so, the law says you may need to make 'reasonable adjustments' so that Topi can keep his job. Check out what is required if you are not sure.

- Make sure you have a method for recording notes from the interview. If you do not have a system in place, search online for 'example Return to Work forms' to see what is typically included.

Steps

- Set Topi at ease and explain the purpose of the meeting.

- Ask about the reasons for the absence.

- Ask him how he feels about returning to work. Address any concerns, also look for underlying issues using questions you've prepared earlier.

- Complete the return to work form, checking for any implications for workplace adjustments as you go.

- Agree any actions or modifications to the workplace needed to help Topi carry out his role, or say you will investigate and get back to him.

- Arrange a follow up meeting if you feel it is necessary to monitor the situation.

Good Practice

There is no hard and fast rule about when, or even if, return to work interviews should be held. Some companies do them after every absence, others if an employee exceeds a certain number of absences in the year, and others only if the absence exceeds a specific length of time. They are popular because they have been shown to be one of the most effective interventions in managing sickness absence; many surveys show that consistently carrying out return to work interviews reduces all forms of absenteeism.

Most large companies have a policy, some smaller companies do them as and when they feel they are necessary. If it is your company, it is worth thinking about what you want your policy to be, and why.

An employer has a duty of care. A return to work interview gives you the chance to welcome your employee back, and to confirm that you have a correct record of their absence and the reasons for it. You also have the opportunity to discuss whether there are any underlying factors you should be aware of.

At the same time the meeting gives Topi the opportunity to raise any remaining health or other issues that he may need your help with, such as modifications to the workplace. It also helps Topi to be accountable for his conduct.

ACAS offer the following guidelines :

- Focus on the health and wellbeing of the employee.
- Be positive and emphasise the value of the employee to the organisation.
- Be careful with the language you use.

So, this should be a constructive conversation that

- smoothes the path of the employee returning to work,
- gives you a better insight into challenges they may be facing and
- builds understanding between you.

Defensiveness and anxieties

Sometimes this interview is a very straightforward task, but it can be more challenging.

For example, it is possible that Topi may be defensive, expecting you to be critical of him, doubting his honesty or 'out to get him'. Remember that defensiveness may mask fear.

You may also be dealing with very sensitive issues that cause Topi to feel anxious about discussing his absence or surrounding factors. He may fear losing his job, or being passed over for promotion.

The best way to lessen defensiveness and anxiety is to make sure you do an excellent job of explaining the purpose of the meeting. Your approach should show that you are being professional, but also approachable and with a genuine interest in Topi's welfare. Allow sufficient time, and use appropriate tone, pace and body language.

Pulling a fast one?

Of course, there is always the possibility that you suspect that Topi is pulling a fast one - or even several fast ones. He may have repeatedly been absent for tenuous, unsubstantiated reasons, causing extra work for disgruntled colleagues.

The thought of being caring and positive in these circumstances may well go against the grain, a natural response may well be to square up for a confrontation.

However...

...the same guidelines apply!

If your primary concern is for the welfare of the individual, you are much more likely to get a positive result.

The relationship between employee and line manager is crucial to gaining commitment and thus good attendance from the individual concerned. Surveys show that employees that have a good relationship with their Line Manager, and who attend a return to work interview, have much lower absence rates (Macleod and Clarke, quoting Gallup 2003).

Think about it. If you are in a grump, what are the chances that the employee is going to feel a new wave of dedication to you or the company? At best, you will get grudging compliance.

To inspire real commitment, you need a real relationship. To build this, it is important to remain objective and listen carefully to what they say. Without this, you are unlikely to tease any concerns from them or get to the heart of the matter.

You will, of course, also be recording the information they give you, and you may have to deliver hard messages - maybe Topi's job is endangered by his absences - but if you put concern about his wellbeing first and foremost you will set the context well.

If Topi is a regular absentee, one approach is asking him to come up with his own action plan to address the problem, to help him take responsibility for his attendance.

If there are difficult things to say, heed the warning below and check your position with an HR professional.

Flexibility

Of course, not all absences are due to sickness. Some are caused by family or other personal issues. If the situation is ongoing, for example childcare, you might want to consider whether it is possible to be flexible about Topi's working hours.

Have a policy

Make sure you have clear procedures in place about how absences should be reported, and a policy about what the consequences will be. This will give you a reference point if you need to discuss absences with Topi.

There are many other strategies you can use to help you manage absence, such as reward schemes and other incentives, so do research further if you need to.

If it is your Return to Work interview...

Be honest! Of course, the employer wants to hear that everything is tickety-boo and that you'll be firing on all cylinders from now on, and hopefully this is the case.

Sometimes, however, there are elements of your work that have contributed to your absence, or you are still not fully fit, so think carefully about what the options are before the meeting, and how you want to say this to your employer.

If you have a health problem or similar, what adjustments can be made to your workplace, and what difference would they make to your productivity and health? Your position needs to be well presented and thought through.

Talk to an HR professional if you need to clarify what support you can reasonably expect from your employer.

Warning!

- This is a book about conversations, not employment law. If you think that you may be going down the path of issuing warnings, or you are not sure to what extent you need to accommodate an individual's health needs, do consult an HR professional to keep you on the straight and narrow. If your organisation isn't large enough to have in-house HR, you can find an HR company who looks after several small companies as and when they are needed. Don't forget to keep complete and accurate records – you may need them.

- Don't make promises you can't carry through. If the employee is asking for changes to the workplace, duties, or other allowances, it is better to say you will get back to them to confirm rather than having to back track, which will damage trust.

- So you think you have a professional and approachable manner? Check the speed you talk at, and your body language. If you speak too fast it can be hard for the other person to break into the conversation. If your body is tense, or your brow furrowed, it won't send the message you are trying to convey. Recording the meeting is important, but the quality of the conversation is more so.

26

Saying Sorry

Definition

Taking steps to repair a broken relationship when there has been fault on your side, apologising, and reaching agreement on how to work together successfully in the future.

Outcomes

- You have honestly admitted the part you played in something going wrong.

- Topi has had an opportunity to tell you how she has been affected by the situation.

- Topi has listened to your apology and hopefully accepts it.

- A discussion has been had about how to put the past behind you and move forward in a way that is acceptable to both sides.

Think Ahead

- What were the triggers that led to the incident? What was down to you, and what was down to other factors?

- What is holding you back from saying sorry?

- Critically evaluate the part you have played. What could you have done differently?

- Do you have a training or development need? If so, how will you address it?

- Does your behaviour need modifying? Does it often lead you into trouble?

- What impact has your mistake or fault had on Topi, the team or the company?

- How important is it that this relationship works?

- How can you put things right?

Steps

- Start by explaining the reason for the apology.

- Say what you are apologising for. Be precise to avoid misunderstanding or assumption, but also sincere and honest.

- Explain how the error occurred, accepting responsibility for your behaviour.

- Acknowledge the consequences of your actions.

- Be prepared to let Topi express her feelings.

- Say how you intend to make amends, and how you will prevent similar incidents happening in the future.

- Ask if there is anything you can do to put things right.

- Ask if your apology is accepted.

Good Practice

The hardest word

We all know that sorry seems to be the hardest word, at least according to Elton John. You may think it is even harder in the workplace, where we are being paid to do a job. Often our natural response to getting it wrong is defensiveness or denial, usually followed by blaming all kinds of outside factors for our own shortcomings.

Too often apologies are clumsy and uncomfortable. Why is this?

- We get embarrassed admitting our mistakes.

- We feel vulnerable showing our weaknesses.

- We try to use forgetting-it-ever-happened as a coping mechanism.

- We experience uncomfortable emotions such as guilt or shame that we would rather avoid.

Humility

You can imagine what it looks like when these feelings get the better of us. There is a danger that we will compensate by bluffing it out, or try to look confident to hide our disappointment in ourselves. This type of behaviour rarely wins us respect.

There is a lot of research around that tells us that the ability to be humble is a key factor in successful leadership. Quiet confidence and the ability to be human wins over loud arrogance and avoidance every time.

Making it easier

You can help to demonstrate your genuineness by:

*   Dealing with it promptly

*   Responding as a human being, not a corporate machine

*   Making eye contact.

You might find that Topi wants to discuss the situation further. This may seem like raking over old coals to you, but she needs to be satisfied that she understands what you are saying, and is reassured that such a thing will not happen again. It's the least you can do.

Lastly... Don't beat yourself up. We are all human and make mistakes from time to time. Part of growing and developing yourself is to get it wrong from time to time – and you will learn far more from your mistakes than your successes.

Once you have owned up and done all you can to rectify the situation, put it behind you and move on. The issue is resolved, so consider it closed.

Now, stop reading about it; go do it.

Warning!

*   Your integrity is at stake if you pass the buck or refuse to take responsibility. Lack of integrity can be the kiss of death on a career.

*   Make sure your apology does not sound like excuses or accusations

*   Don't say *"...but...".*

27

Supervisory Meetings

Definition

A regular, informal meeting between a line manager and his subordinate, often called a "*One to one*".

These discussions keep both informed, and allow them to discuss any difficulties, agree action points and monitor progress. The objective is to keep Topi motivated and engaged in her work.

Outcomes

- The line manager has had the opportunity to discuss how Topi's work is going and to monitor progress.

- Topi has had the opportunity to raise any work based concerns she has, and share her successes.

- Potential issues have been discussed and resolved.

- Forthcoming work and projects have been planned and action points agreed.

- The relationship between Topi and her manager is strengthened.

Think Ahead

- What motivates Topi to perform well?

- How has Topi performed since your last meeting? Are you basing your opinion on direct evidence or hearsay?

- Is she working to her potential? If not, what obstacles is she facing? How could they be overcome?

- Are then any upcoming projects or events that you need to discuss with her?

- Is there anything you can delegate to help enhance her skills or gain more experience?

- What praise and encouragement can you give her?

- Do you need to know in advance what Topi wants to discuss?

Steps

- **Ask Topi if there are any issues in particular she wants to discuss.** Add any topics you want to bring up, and then prioritise the items on your list.

- **Review the period of work and progress on action points** since your last meeting. Let Topi lead the way and give her thoughts first. You can listen, agree and confirm or clarify as appropriate, and put things in perspective if necessary.

- **Work through the items on your list**, asking Topi for comments and ideas. You will get more buy in for Topi's own suggestions rather than yours. Let her know you value her input even if you can't act on her ideas.

- **Give Topi some feedback on her work** if it hasn't come up already. You can also give her feedback on her attitude, and how it impacts on others. If you want her to behave differently, make sure you can describe how you want her to act as well as what you don't want.

- **Discuss any learning and development needs Topi may have**. Review any training she may have done and help her implement it.

- **Ask if she has any feedback for you,** or anything else she wants to raise.

- **Agree a time and place for your next meeting**.

Good Practice

One to ones are very common practice as a method of keeping the flow of communication open between a manager and the individual staff in the team.

For many they work well, helping to build a strong working relationship, which is a crucial part of getting the best out of Topi. Other managers struggle to know how to make the best use of them, even resenting the time it takes out of a busy diary. Which camp are you in?

What drives Topi?

The bottom line is that we want Topi to work to the best of her ability, being a productive and motivated member of the team.

To achieve this, many factors are involved, but an understanding of what drives Topi is critical to success. Many motivating factors are common to nearly all of us, like those Maslow identified and mentioned in the chapter on Praising: a sense of belonging, feeling a part of a team, being respected, and having status.

Other factors are unique to the individual, and also fluctuate as we go through different life stages. We may or may not be driven by money, or ambition, or being able to create new things, or working with like-minded folk.

The question is, what is it that makes Topi get out of bed in the mornings? A good line manager will do his best to understand what motivates Topi, and adapt his approach to her accordingly.

Be flexible

Some organisations use a uniform format to help managers treat staff consistently, which is likely to be based on something like the Steps at the start of this chapter. There are examples online if you would like to see how other organisations do it.

You can have a set format if you find this helpful, but a degree of flexibility is also useful to meet the challenges at work and changes that take Topi outside her comfort zone. In these cases Topi could do with a bit more support and encouragement; Topi's needs are more important than a rigid format.

Several of the other chapters in this book may be helpful and relevant here, such as Coaching, Challenging, Delegating or Praising depending on what is going on in your workplace.

Record keeping

It's a good idea to keep notes from your supervisory meetings. They need only be brief, but they should mention the key points discussed, agreed action, and anything carried over until next time.

They should also be transparent – let Topi see them so she can say if she thinks anything is missing or incorrect.

They will also help you to prepare for appraisals when you will need to look back over the year to review Topi's performance.

If it is your supervisory meeting...

Take the opportunity to let your boss know what you have done well, and how you have overcome difficulties and dealt with problems effectively.

This may or may not come naturally, and you don't want to be boastful, but you should make a realistic assessment of the contribution you have made.

Why is it important to do this?

Often people get promoted not because they have done good work, but because **their manager knows** they do good work – you can not assume that keeping your head down and working diligently will be noticed by the people who influence decisions. Do your own PR.

Warning!

- One to one meetings are often put on the back burner because there are no urgent issues to discuss, in the view of the manager, at least. If you keep postponing them, what messages are you sending to Topi? She may feel that her contribution is unimportant, that your time is more precious than hers, or that you have no interest in how things are going for her. Is that the message you want to send? If you do cancel, apologise.

- Are you going through the motions because it is company policy, rather than taking a genuine interest? If so you can easily demotivate Topi.

- If you make the notes from your supervisory as formal as meeting minutes they will hardly be inspiring.

28

Giving 360° Feedback

Definition

A meeting to help Topi understand and accept the contents of a 360° report, which contains feedback from Topi's superiors, colleagues and subordinates. The meeting puts the report into context and identifies Topi's key strengths and development needs in the view of the respondents.

Outcomes

- Topi has increased self awareness, and has learnt how his colleagues perceive him.

- Topi has had the opportunity to reflect on the implications of the report.

- Development points and topics for further investigation have been identified.

- You are satisfied that you have offered appropriate support and challenges to help Topi get the maximum benefit from both the report and the feedback meeting.

Think Ahead

- Analyse the report, identifying the main themes, inconsistencies, perception gaps, strengths, and key development areas.

- Prepare the questions you want to ask and the topics you think need to be discussed.

- If there are any potentially upsetting points, think through the possible reactions and how you will handle them.

- Remember this meeting is about Topi's development, not what you think he should do. What will you do to ensure you remain impartial and supportive?

Steps

- **Explain your role as a facilitator** (as above) and other ground rules and boundaries, e.g. how long the session will last, confidentiality, who will see the report, and what will happen if Topi needs more support than you can offer.

- **Work through the report**, letting Topi take the lead. Your job here is to help Topi make sense of it and make sure that he has taken the important points on board. It is usually good to start with the overview at the beginning, which most reports have. After that, you can either go through the sections in the order they appear, or let Topi choose which he wants to discuss first.

- **Be alert to Topi's reactions**. Is he picking up themes and linking items? Is he realistic, over dramatising, or being dismissive? Guide and gently challenge where you need to.

- **Ask Topi to summarise his learning and thoughts**, and what action points he intends to take.

- **Flesh out the action points as far as possible.** Some may need further research to find the best way forward.

- **End the meeting on a positive note.** Most of us have an inclination to dwell on the negative, so make sure Topi has a balanced view and does not forget his strengths.

Good Practice

What is 360° feedback?

360° feedback is an established development tool that has been adopted by many organisations with considerable success.

If you have not come across it, it is an online system which starts with Topi assessing himself against a set of competences online. A group of Topi's colleagues, typically 8-10, are also invited to complete the same questionnaire about Topi. These colleagues are selected from above, below and at the same level as Topi, e.g. his line manager or subordinates reporting to him, colleagues in other departments that he works with regularly. Most of the questions are scored, usually on a scale of 1-5, followed by a couple of free text questions, such as *"What does this person do well and should do more of?"*, or *"What should this person stop doing or change?"*

As soon as sufficient people have answered the questionnaire, a report is generated that shows the information gathered in a variety of formats, for example bar charts and spidergrams. It can be a lot of data to take in, so it is good practice for someone who is familiar with the tool, and has some coaching skills, to help Topi through it.

Selecting a 360° questionnaire

You may be involved in setting up the 360° feedback. There are a lot of different versions on the market, so do your homework as they vary considerably. Most suppliers have sample reports that you can download. Look for:

- **Quality.** Does it seem to be a tried and trusted, professional tool?

- **Flexibility.** Can you adapt it to suit your job roles or competency framework? There is little point if you are measuring the wrong things. Can you choose whether you take care of the administration or the supplier does it for you?

- **Ease of use**. Is the online system straightforward and easy to understand?

- **Presentation of the report**. Is it well laid out, attractive and easy to follow?

- **Workbook.** Good tools have a workbook that will help Topi analyse the report, and can help you to structure the feedback meeting.

- **Support.** Is there good technical back up to answer your queries speedily in plain English? Can they provide trained coaches to either do the feedback for you, or train your staff to do it?

All of these are important factors to take into account if you are to get the best from the tool.

Before the meeting

One consideration is whether you give the report to Topi before the meeting, of if he sees it for the first time on the day. There is no hard and fast rule.

Some people prefer the first approach, so that there is more time in the feedback meeting to discuss the learning and the action points, while others prefer to bring it fresh to the meeting. The only caveat here is that if you can see that a report is likely to be taken badly it is probably better to be with Topi when he receives it, rather than let him fret about it until the meeting.

Another consideration is who should conduct the feedback meeting. It is not best practice for Topi's line manager to do this, as it is hard for a manager to take an impartial, objective approach when they have their own opinion on how Topi performs.

Some of the comments or scores may touch on sensitive issues or come as bad news to Topi, for example if he discovers that he is not as well respected as he thought. It is important that the person giving the feedback is able to cope with situations like these.

If you feel it is outside your expertise it is best to get someone appropriately trained to do it.

During the meeting

Your role is to focus your attention on helping Topi. This means helping him to keep things in perspective, being constructive, and assisting him in identifying the action points that will have most impact.

To do this well you have to remain impartial, and find out what is going on around him in the workplace at the moment so you have a context. You'll also need to know what is important to him, his initial response to the report and what areas he would like to concentrate on. At this stage you will have more questions than answers, so be aware that any conclusions you have drawn by reading the report in advance may seem different once you have heard Topi's context and explanation. Be prepared to change your mind, and express all views tentatively.

Topi should be encouraged to take their lead on the discussion, but do challenge if you think he is deliberately avoiding important or obvious issues. You may have also an emotional response to deal with, so allow Topi space to get his emotions off his chest if you need to. Be supportive, but challenge overreactions and point out the positives.

To be as effective as possible you should:

- Have a repertoire of coaching style questions to get to the heart of the matter, e.g. *"What makes you say that?," "What would you like to be different?", "Where do you want to be?", "How could you reach your goals?", "What steps do you need to take first?".* Have a look at the Coaching chapter for more suggestions.

- Manage the time effectively, and revisit and adjust the agreed priorities if you need to. Don't get bogged down in the detail.

- Try and end with a manageable handful of action points – too many will be demoralising and get lost.

- Have a discussion around how the action points will be achieved, any support that is necessary, and any potential obstacles to be overcome.

- If Topi has issues that you cannot deal with, e.g. outside of your skills and experience – do not try. Be prepared to signpost them to someone who can help.

After the meeting

- Reflect on your own performance. Did it go well? Is there anything you could have done differently? Anything you missed out? How can you do it better next time?

- Plug any skill gaps you find by training, researching, or asking more experienced colleagues to help you practise different techniques.

If it is your 360 report...

Often, when introducing 360° feedback, companies work from the top down, so you may well find that you have your own report to deal with before your team have theirs. Do prepare for your feedback meeting (use the workbook if you have one) by suspending defensiveness, genuinely trying to understand why you have received the feedback, and what the key learning points are for you.

Warning!

- Who will get to see Topi's report? Or know what was discussed? If Topi is to be able to discuss issues freely and with confidence everyone needs to know what is confidential. Make sure the processes are transparent.

- If you already have a system for setting learning and development objectives it could get messy if you introduce 360° feedback without thinking about how it fits in with existing processes.

Bibliography

- ACAS (2006) *Advisory Booklet – Managing Attendance and Employee Turnover* ACAS

- ACAS (2009) *Code of Practice - Disciplinary and Grievance Procedures* ACAS

- Blanchard, Kenneth, and Johnson, Spencer (1994) *The One Minute Manager* Harper Collins

- De Bono, Edward (1994) *De Bono's Thinking Course* BBC

- Cooper, Julie, and Reynolds, Ann (2008) *The One to One Toolkit* Careertrain Publishing

- Egan, Gerard (2001) *The Skilled Helper: A Problem-Management and Opportunity-Development Approach to Helping* Wadsworth

- Fisher, Roger, and Ury, William (1991) *Getting to Yes - Negotiating an Agreement without Giving In* Random House

- French, J. R. P., Raven, B. (1959) *The bases of social power* in D. Cartwright and A. Zander. Group dynamics. New York: Harper & Row

- Gillen, Terry (2001) *Agreed! Improve your Powers of Influence* CIPD

- Goldstein, Noah J., Martin, Steve J., and Cialdini, Robert (1997) *Yes! 50 Secrets from the Science of Persuasion* Profile Books

- Heron, John (1989) *Six Category Intervention Analysis* Human Potential Resource Group

- Honey, Peter (1997) *Improve your People Skills* IPD

- Honey, Peter, and Mumford, Alan (1986) *Manual of Learning Styles* Peter Honey Publications

- Kolb, David A. (1984) *Experiential Learning: Experience as the source of learning and development* Englewood Cliffs, N.J.: Prentice Hall

- Kübler Ross, Elisabeth (1997) *On Death and Dying* Scribner

- Macleod, David, and Clarke, Nita (2009) *Engaging for Success: Enhancing performance through employee engagement* Department of Business, Innovation and Skills

- Maslow, Abraham (1987) *Motivation and Personality* Harper and Row

- Robbins, Anthony (1989) *Unlimited Power* Simon and Schuster Ltd

- Rogers, Carl (1967) *On becoming a Person* Constable and Company Ltd

- Senge, Peter (1993) *The Fifth Discipline* Random House Business

- Ury, William (2007) *Getting to Yes* Profile Books Ltd

- Whitmore, John (2002) *Coaching for Performance* Nicholas Brierley Publishing

Index